Learning the Skills Of Anger Management

Ready-to-use Lessons
for the Elementary Grades

Terri Akin

FREE After School Resource Catalog
School-Age NOTES
P.O. Box 40205
Nashville, TN 37204
1-800-410-8780
www.AfterSchoolCatalog.com

Write to: Jalmar Press
P.O. Box 1185
Torrance, CA 90505
Email: blwjalmar@worldnet.att.net
Tel: (310)816-3085 Fax: (310)816-3092

ISBN: 1-880396-94-7

Printed in the United States of America

Printing #: 10 9 8 7 6 5 4 3 2 1

Learning the Skills of Anger Management
Ready-to-Use Lessons for the Elementary Grades

Table of Contents

Learning the Skills of Anger Management
Ready-to-Use Lessons for the Elementary Grades

Introduction

"The angry man will defeat himself in battle as well as in life."

Everyone gets angry. It's a normal emotion that we all experience throughout our lives. It can range from slight annoyance or minor irritation to full-blown rage. It can result from real or perceived injury, not getting what we want, and other stressful situations. Anger is difficult to hide. At the height of anger, faces may become flushed, breathing may accelerate, facial expressions become tight or contorted, the pitch of the voice rises, and body language reveals a defensive mode or closing down of communication. Anger may spur us to strike out verbally with accusations, sarcasm or insults, or physically, by slamming doors, throwing things, kicking furniture or hitting another person. We can also react to anger passively, by withdrawing into silence.

When I was a kindergarten teacher, I remember a child who got very angry because he didn't get his way while playing a game on the rug with a small group of his classmates. He began to scream at the top of his lungs, then he grabbed a large wooden building block about his own size and hurled it with amazing strength at the other children. Luckily, his aim was not as good as his strength, and he did not harm any of his classmates. I was a young, naive teacher at the time, and I scolded him while marching him to the office for timeout and principal's consequences. I had not yet learned to acknowledge the child's feelings of anger because I was so frightened by his behavior.

I have seen many other instances in my 26 years of teaching in grades K through six. On more than one occasion I have put the short-tempered and misbehaving student next to a quiet, kind student in the classroom, thinking that the influence of the well-behaved one would rub off on the one who acted out. The well-behaved student would complain very little, if at all. But on more than one occasion, I got a call from one of the parents of that student with concerns that the child, who previously loved school, no longer wanted to come. It took awhile for me to figure out that the child was really angry about being put next to the student who acted out. Because the well-behaved student didn't feel comfortable about expressing her anger, I never knew how annoyed and harassed she felt. She just held it in and became disenchanted with school.

1

Like myself, every elementary classroom teacher has had children in their classes who express their anger in inappropriate ways: biting, hitting, kicking, scratching, destroying property, verbal abuse and surreptitious behaviors such as stealing and lying. We have set out our expectations in the form of classroom rules and followed them up with consequences. These are very effective ways to manage behavior in the classroom. However, the students need to learn effective ways to control, express and release their anger on their own in order to become empowered, responsible, contributing members of the school, their peer groups and families. This is the road to becoming responsible, compassionate and contributing citizens of our society and the global community.

Perhaps in using these activities as a teaching tool in the classroom, we can prevent some of the inappropriate, and sometimes violent, "acting out" by those students who lack inner controls. With a heightened awareness, the quiet, well-behaved student can feel safe about voicing his or her anger at what appears an injustice. Learning together makes it easier because we can create a common language and understanding of the concepts of anger management. The students can become each other's teachers, coaching each other and practicing the skills until they become automatic.

The purposes of this book are to:

1. Explain in simple terms the nature of anger — what causes it and how it affects us physiologically, emotionally and mentally.
2. Make clear the role of thoughts, attitudes, beliefs and perceptions in controlling and releasing anger.
3. Present and explore components of an anger-management program.
4. Offer activities within each component that you can use to assist your children to develop a repertoire of anger-management skills.

Impulsive or aggressive behavior in response to anger is not uncommon, particularly in children. You've probably often observed the effects anger has on how receptive children are to teaching and learning in the classroom. Unbridled anger disrupts thinking and distorts behavior. It impairs a child's ability to make accurate judgments and to recall information. It can severely damage peer relations and lead to disciplinary action, delivering walloping blows to self-esteem.

Children are often told to ignore their anger. When they cannot ignore it, they are expected to control it, but they are rarely shown how to do so. Consciously or unconsciously, children realize that we all experience anger. On television, anger and violence are inexorably linked, yet we admonish children not to fight, physically or verbally.

Adults often struggle with anger and fail to express or even admit it. Why? Many of us were trained as children that it was not OK to be angry, and it was unacceptable to express anger in any way. Many of us were made to feel guilty for showing anger, as if it were a bad behavior. It is a common myth in our society that anger is not good and should be eliminated. But we know it can't be. As we have matured into adulthood, most of us have learned to acknowledge, control and often release anger in spite of the discomfort of doing so. We know that if we try to suppress it, it will come out in other ways. Anger management has become a skill learned by experience, i.e. trial and error.

"The holiest of all the spots on earth is where ancient hatred has become a present love."

Dealing with children's anger can also be distressing, frustrating and puzzling for adults. This is because our own anger is stirred up as the child "acts out" her anger. We remember how our own caregivers treated us in these situations, and we want to handle them differently, with more compassion and fairness. But we wonder how to do so. We also are afraid of anger because it may mean that someone is out of control. Domestic violence, TV violence and road rage are contemporary examples of anger gone out of control. From the violence we see and hear on a daily basis, we know that angry outbursts aren't very productive. Yet we have also learned that bottling up anger can create depression and illness.

How do we, as teachers, counselors and parents, help children control and manage anger and upset inside and out of the classroom? How do we teach them that getting mad is OK and that there are healthy, effective ways to express, manage and release anger? We don't want to leave it to chance or temporary "Band-Aid" approaches. First and foremost, we begin by modeling appropriate anger management. As the old adage goes, "Children learn by example." Then we must move from where the child is into the direction of appropriate, acceptable behaviors through strategies directly taught, practiced, and practiced some more until they become automatic. Just as we would not expect children to learn musical instruments without massive amounts of practice, we must allow time and repetition to cultivate and solidify anger-management skills.

This book presents activities that address strategies elementary school children can learn in order to manage their anger in a variety of situations. These activities encompass the diverse learning modes and "multiple intelligences" that children possess. The activities should be enjoyed, and yet taken seriously. Each child is on the learning curve of emotional development and will grasp the concepts at her own level. Patience, persistence and consistency on the part of the adult are critical and will reap their own rewards.

As adult caregivers, we must keep in mind that some children come to us from homes that have not supported their social and emotional development. Physical, sexual, verbal and other emotional abuse may be obstacles and deterrents to children learning the skills they need to control their behaviors. Hours of TV viewing and video games in which violence plays a major role take their toll on the speed at which children can internalize the healthy, life-changing concepts of anger management. Individual personalities and developmental stages are important factors that also must be considered. Some children may require more intervention, practice and monitoring than others. A child who displays violent behaviors consistently or who appears depressed may need additional professional help. However, the activities in this book can serve as a springboard to their healing and help create behavior changes.

The activities in this book are designed to assist and train children to acknowledge, accept and manage their anger. As children learn to deal with their anger, they will feel more in control of their lives. It is a step toward positive and powerful self-esteem. Have fun with this guide and allow the children you work with to dive into the activities, exhibit their own creativity, and grow at their own pace. Look for the small steps that each child makes on the path to developing and internalizing an anger-management system. Above all, have faith in yourself as a facilitator, and trust the process.

Basic Concepts

The concepts and premises upon which the activities in this book were created include the following:

Anger is a normal, healthy human emotion and, as such is OK.

Anger serves as a signal and can protect us.

The feeling is not the same as the behavior.

It is how we react to a situation, not the situation itself, that causes our anger.

It is not OK to hurt yourself, another person or anyone's property.

Anger is generally not the problem, the mismanagement of it is.

Thoughts come before feelings, therefore we can become aware of the feelings created by our thoughts.

If we can change our mind about something, we may be able to change the feeling.

We have choices as to how we react to any situation.

Anger can be used to positively motivate us.

Underlying issues that create anger include issues of power, capabilities, fairness and recognition.

It is good to learn the language that can identify and express anger.

There are healthy ways to express anger.

There are healthy ways to release anger.

Movement can assist in calming feelings and focusing thoughts.

Deep breathing can help calm and dissipate anger.

Repressed anger may become explosive.

Repressed anger can be harmful to one's health.

Stating what you feel, why you feel it and what you want is a healthy way to become assertive.

Each of us is responsible for our own feelings and behavior.

How to Use This Book

This book is divided into five sections: Understanding anger, Expressing Anger, Managing Anger, Releasing Anger, and Literature Connections. Each of the first four sections begins with two "Sharing Circles" and contains a variety of activities and a culminating worksheet. The chapters can be taken in any order, depending on the developmental level and needs of the students. You can pick and choose from the activities in any given chapter, but it is helpful to conduct the Sharing Circles first in order to connect the children's life experiences with the new things they learn.

The Sharing Circle

The Sharing Circle is an organized discussion format that encourages spontaneous sharing in response to a given TOPIC. No two Sharing Circles are the same, even with the same topic, because every participant brings a different set of views and experiences to the process. The topics in this guide allow children to explore the subject of anger with one another, to appreciate themselves and others as developing persons, to practice communication skills, and to develop empathy with others.

The objectives of the Sharing Circle are to increase children's understanding of themselves, their self-esteem and sense of social responsibility, and to create a bridge from the children's set of knowledge and experiences to the desired skills. To achieve these objectives, the Sharing Circle uses a circular, small-group (of six to 12) seating arrangement; ground rules that set the tone for personal privacy and safety; and a procedural structure that invites each child to share, give reflective feedback and cognitively summarize what he or she has learned.

This discussion group is an activity just like others in the book, with desired objectives and outcomes. As such, there are procedures to follow and rules of conduct to guarantee that the objectives have the best opportunity to be met. As the leader of the Sharing Circle, you state

"'I lose my temper, but it's all over in a minute,' said the student. 'So is the hydrogen bomb,' I replied, 'but think of the damage it produces.'"

and enforce these simple rules of considerate conduct, model your own respect for those rules, lead the discussion, and listen carefully to what the children say. The steps for conducting the Sharing Circle include:

1. **Set the tone.** Be enthusiastic, smile, use eye contact and gestures to let the children feel welcome in the group. Make sure that you are sitting in a circle so everyone can be seen.

2. **Review the Sharing Circle Rules:**

   Bring yourself, and nothing else, to the circle.

   Everyone, including the leader, gets one turn to share.

   We don't have to take a turn if we don't want to.

   We share the time equally.

   We listen to the person who is speaking.

   We stay in our own space and keep our hands and feet to ourselves.

   We don't interrupt or put down another person.

3. **Introduce the topic and elaborate on the topic.** State the topic first, and then take a minute to clarify what the session is about and give examples of possible responses so that the children can get some ideas for their responses. Restate the topic. Then provide a few seconds of quiet thinking time before opening up to sharing.

4. **Give each child who takes a turn about one minute to share.** It is important that this portion of the time be completely free of judgment, advice or any other sort of distracting or negating comments, even if the children copy each other's responses or make up unrealistic stories.

5. **Optional: Conduct a review (approximately half a minute per participant).** This step offers the children who contributed a chance to hear other circle members tell them what they heard them share. Its purpose is to sharpen listening and observation skills, to give circle members another chance to participate verbally, and to assure children who spoke that they were

listened to. Keep in mind that this is offered at your discretion.

6. **Lead a summary.** Ask an open-ended question to stimulate thought and free discussion regarding the concepts, lessons and other connections that can be made as a result of the sharing. This meets the needs of everyone involved to find meaning in the discussion. Each Sharing Circle in this book includes two or more summary questions; however, you may want to formulate questions that are more appropriate to the level of understanding of your students. Do not confuse the summary with the review. The review is optional; the summary is not. The summary serves as a necessary culmination to each Sharing Circle by allowing the children to clarify the key concepts gained from the session.

7. **Close the circle.** Thank the children for their cooperation, sharing and listening. Announce that the circle is over.

"Brain Gym" ™

Some of the activities in this guide are taken from the book "Brain Gym" (1986) by Paul E. Dennison, Ph.D., a pioneer in applied brain research, and Gail Dennison, and are used with permission. "Brain Gym" is based on whole-brain learning, kinesiology, movement repatterning, "Touch for Health" and other types of sensorimotor training. The movement repatterning in "Brain Gym" activities enables students to access those parts of the brain previously inaccessible to them. "Brain Gym" activities were found to stimulate, release or relax students involved in particular learning situations. "Brain Gym" is a registered trademark of the Educational Kinesiology Foundation, Ventura, Calif.

Understanding Anger

Anger is a normal, universal emotion. This segment focuses student attention on understanding the various aspects of anger: its internal and external physical manifestations, the language used to describe intensities of anger, its causes, and underlying issues or fears. The aim is to make children more aware and accepting of their anger and to lead them to further exploration of anger management.

Sharing Circle:
A Time I Was Really Angry

Sharing Circle:
A Time I Noticed That Someone Was Angry

Discussion and Art:
If It Looks Like Angry, It Probably Is

Brainstorm and Role-Play:
From Mad to Worse: Measuring Anger

Discussion and Chart:
Things I Get Angry About

Worksheet:
What Lit My Fuse?

A Time I Was Really Angry
Sharing Circle

Objectives:

— To become aware of the feelings and reactions of our bodies when we are angry.

— To understand the variety of internal and external symptoms of anger in different people.

— To understand that we all experience anger in one form or another.

Directions:

Ask the children to form a circle, and introduce or go over the ground rules (See: How to Use This Book — Sharing Circles, page 6). If the rules have already been introduced, ask the circle members to say a rule they remember until all the rules are covered. Add any that they may have forgotten.

Introduce the Topic: "Today we are going to talk about 'A Time I Was Really Angry.'"

Elaborate: "Think of a time when you were really mad, more than annoyed or irritated; you were furious. Choose a time you feel OK about sharing with the group. It could be when you felt someone treated you unfairly, or when you were angry with yourself for dropping or breaking something. Think about how you felt inside your body. Were you breathing heavily, or was your stomach turning somersaults? Did you clench your teeth, tighten your lips or get red in the face? How was your voice? Did you growl or shriek? Did you stomp your feet or kick something? Focus on what it felt like inside your body and how you reacted with your body. Do not use any names. It is not important to know who you were mad at. You can say 'a friend' or 'someone I know.' Take a few moments to think about how your body showed that you were angry. The topic is 'A Time I Was Really Angry.' "

Begin the sharing: Invite the children to take turns speaking. Listen carefully to each one and encourage the other children to do the same. Don't allow interruptions. Be sure to take a turn yourself.

"I am often mad, but I would hate to be nothing but mad."

E. B. White

Optional: After everyone who wants a turn has had one, ask if anyone can remember what another has said. Allow the children to tell each other what they've heard. Acknowledge them for good listening.

■ Summary:

After each child who wants to speak has done so, ask the following questions:

— *How do our bodies react when we are angry?*
— *Why do you think it is important to notice what our bodies do when we are angry?*

A Time I Noticed That Someone Was Angry
Sharing Circle

Objectives:

— To recognize the symptoms of anger in other people. To understand how we feel in reaction to other people's anger.

Directions:

Invite the children to form a circle and introduce or go over the ground rules. If the rules were already introduced, ask the circle members to repeat a rule that they recall until all the rules have been restated. Be sure to add any that have been forgotten.

Note: This topic may be less intimidating for some students to begin the study of anger management. It tends to be a good icebreaker for a group whose members don't know each other well.

Introduce the Topic: "In this Sharing Circle, we are going to share about 'A Time I Noticed That Someone Was Angry.'"

Elaborate: "Everyone gets angry. It's a normal emotion. We have all seen other people get angry in many ways. Today, I want you to think of a time when you noticed that someone else was angry. Don't use any names. You can say, 'This boy ... or girl' or 'an adult' or 'a person in the grocery store.' It could have been someone on television. You may not have seen the person at all. Maybe you heard him or her yelling at someone or crying angrily. How did it sound to you? It could have been someone you saw but didn't hear. Their face may have shown that they were mad. How did they show they were angry? How did it make YOU feel? Did it make you angry? Did your body react to their anger? Were you scared? Did you laugh nervously? Did you get away from the situation? Don't say anyone's name, just focus on what the person looked like and/or sounded like, and how you felt, as well. Let's spend a moment to reflect on the topic, 'A Time I Noticed That Someone Was Angry.'"

Begin the Sharing: Announce that the circle is open for sharing and that we all need to pay attention to the person speaking. Make sure that each person has an opportunity to share but may pass on it if they wish. If children are reluctant to begin the sharing, volunteer to be the first to talk. This often breaks the ice.

"There are good and bad times, but our mood changes more often than our fortune."

Jules Renard

Optional: If you want to allow students to repeat back what each other has said, this is an opportunity for them to learn by repeating what they hear. Active listening often anchors a fleeting concept, story or new learning. Also, showing other people that you have heard what they said by repeating it back acknowledges their contributions to the group.

 Summary:

    After the sharing is complete, conduct a summary by asking some open-ended questions like these:

— *How do people sometimes look when they are angry?*
— *What do people sometimes sound like when they are angry?*
— *How does other people's anger make us feel?*
— *Why might it be important to get away from some people who are angry?*

Additional Topics: If you want to conduct more Sharing Circles, or use different, but related, topics, try these: "What I Did When I Was Angry," "What I Saw Someone Do When Angry," "A Time I Read About (Or Saw On TV) A Person Who Was Angry," or "I Didn't Say A Word, But They Knew I Was Angry."

If It Looks Like Angry, It Probably Is
Discussion and Art

"There is not in nature, a thing that makes man so deformed, so beastly, as doth intemperate anger."

John Webster

Objective:

— To understand the nonverbal clues, i.e., body language, that indicate anger in people.

Materials needed:

Pictures of angry people on the next two pages, whiteboard with markers or chalkboard with chalk, white construction paper, markers, crayons or colored pencils, Post-it notes, pencils, CD or tape player, CDs or audio tapes of music that would accompany an angry feeling, such as parts of the "1812 Overture" by Tchaikovsky, "The Storm" from Grofe's "Grand Canyon Suite," "Mars" from "The Planets" by Gustav Holst, or any "acid rock" or "heavy metal" music that has loud, discordant sounds.

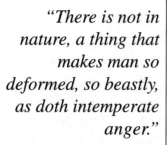

Directions:

1. Show the pictures on the following two pages of the people who are angry. Ask the students, "What do you notice about the people in the pictures?" Answers may vary but should include comments such as, "The people look mad," "Everyone is angry," "They don't look too happy," and "I wonder what made them so angry."

2. Elicit a discussion on why the students think that each person is mad. You might say to them, "Pretend you are detectives and you must think of what evidence shows anger in each picture. Look at the face and body. What do you notice?" Write the word "Evidence" on the board as a heading. Then list the physical characteristics that the children see as evidence in the pictures. Have them add any other physical characteristics they might see in angry people. Included in the list might be narrowed eyes, clenched fists, scrunched-up face, red face, sweat, arms crossed over the stomach, tight lips, hands on hips, stomping foot, bared teeth or head held forward.

3. Distribute the art paper and markers, crayons or colored pencils. Explain to the students that they will draw a picture of an angry person showing some of the evidence that was listed on the board. Suggest that they show as many physical characteristics as they can in their picture.

4. Allow 15 to 25 minutes for this part of the activity. During the activity, you may want to play some "angry" music. Explain that this is music to inspire their interpretations of anger.

5. When the pictures are completed, put a Post-it note on each picture and conduct a "walk-around" in which the students file around the tables and look at each other's pictures. As they do, ask them to write on the Post-it note what features of each picture show evidence of anger. Each person may write only one feature and cannot repeat what another has written for a particular picture.

Summary:

When the "walk-around" is complete, conduct a brief summary of the activity. Suggest that the children think again about what they notice when they see people angry and then ask:

— *What are some of the kinds of evidence that someone is angry?*
— *How do you think it would help you to notice when someone else is angry?*

Guide the students to understand that being able to "read" other people's emotions, to attend to nonverbal cues, is a survival skill. We can avoid confrontation with people who show they are angry by keeping our distance from them or being extra nice to them.

From Mad to Worse: Measuring Anger
Brainstorm and Role-Play

Objectives:

To understand that there are degrees of anger, from mild to intense. To learn the language that describes the varying degrees of anger.

Materials Needed:

Whiteboard or chalkboard, pens or chalk, pencils and paper.

Directions:

1. Bring the students together, and ask them if they can think of any synonyms, or words that mean the same, as anger. Depending on their age level, students may contribute words such as "mad," "annoyed," "irritated," "grumpy," "ticked-off," "upset," "cranky," "grouchy," "furious," "violent" or "resentful." You may add to the list a few extras for language development, such as "agitated," "enraged," "livid," "irate," "aggravated," "wrathful," "indignant," "piqued" or "provoked." Explain the nuances of the words you add. Ask volunteers to show what each word would look like in body language and facial expression.

2. Explain that each label for anger suggests a certain degree of anger, from mild to boiling hot. Tell the students that they can measure how angry someone is and describe it by using one of the words. Ask the students to work in groups of four to six to rank the angry words from what to them is just mild anger (a little angry) to boiling hot (BIG angry). Although there will be no exactly right or wrong ranking, guide the groups to think about each word and their experience of it. Ask them to come to a consensus on their list. If you are working with younger children, you may do this activity with the whole class or group.

"We boil at different degrees."

Ralph Waldo Emerson

3. When the groups are finished, gather them into the big group and ask them to share their rankings with the class. Then ask if there are any patterns among the lists. Draw a simple diagram of a thermometer on the board with a vertical stem attached to a bulb at the bottom and add lines indicating measurements. Have the class come to a general consensus on the words indicating degrees of anger. Add your input if the interpretations seem inaccurate. You may start with the milder words such as "grumpy," "cranky," "annoyed" or "irritated," and move up the scale to "upset," "aggravated," "mad," "angry," "ticked-off" and "irate." The top of the scale would probably have the words "furious," "enraged," "livid," "wrathful" and "violent."

4. Invite the students to divide into pairs or small groups and think of a situation in which they could role-play to demonstrate one of the degrees of anger. For example, two children may act out a scenario in which one person takes his partner's pencil when he can't find his own. One person may act out a time when he forgot his homework on the kitchen table and, as a result, lost his recess the next day. Have the class "measure" the degree of anger that is shown in the scenario and guess one of the words on the thermometer that matches the intensity of that anger. Have them explain why they chose a certain word. Remind the students that they may personally feel a greater or lesser degree of anger in someone else's scenario, but they are just observing the intensity acted out in the role-play.

Summary:

Have the students do a silent summary of the activity by asking them to close their eyes while you read each word and visualize a situation in which they felt or would feel each of the degrees of anger. Allow five to 10 seconds between each word. Explain that using certain words to describe how angry we are helps us to share our feelings more accurately with someone else.

Things I Get Angry About
Discussion and Chart

Objectives:

— To explore the causes of our anger.
— To understand the causes of anger as oriented toward other people, situations, actions or self.
— To understand what categories trigger our anger the most.

Materials Needed:

Whiteboard with markers or chalkboard with chalk.

Directions:

"How much more grievous are the consequences of anger than the causes of it."

Marcus Aurelius

1. Gather the children together and elicit a discussion about why people get angry. Ask them: "What causes people to get angry? Why do you get angry? Is it a certain kind of person, like someone who always hums to him/herself? Is it yourself because you make simple mistakes on your homework or on a test? Or are you angry that you cannot hit a baseball as well as you would like? Could it be a situation in which you got hurt or something you own was damaged? Perhaps you get mad when you don't get your way or you don't get something you want. It might be a situation in which you have to wait a long time in line to get something." Elicit answers. Make sure that no names are given with respect to people. Reassure the children that not everyone gets mad at the same kind of person or situation.

2. Write the following headings on the board: *People, Situations, Self,* and *Actions.* Make a column for each. If the students are old enough, give a different colored whiteboard marker to each of four volunteers. Have each student stand in front of a column.

3. Then say, "Let's take the examples that you shared and put them in a category on this chart. The category, *People,* means certain types of people, such as those who are really loud or who laugh at everything or drop garbage on the sidewalk. *Situations* are specific things that seem to happen to you, like

when you have to finish an extra-long homework assignment instead of watching a favorite TV show, when it rains for five days in a row and you can't go out and play, or when your bike gets a flat tire. *Self* means yourself. These are things about you that always make you mad, like being clumsy or not having curly hair. *Actions* are things that anyone or anything could do to annoy you, like when a dog barks at you as you are rollerblading down the sidewalk. It might be anytime someone cuts in line ahead of you, or when someone takes your pen or pencil from your desk at school."

4. As the students review their examples and think of additional ones, ask the group to decide on a category in which to place them and have the volunteers write them under the appropriate category. Invite them to notice what makes them angry the most: certain types of people, situations, themselves or actions. Explain that knowing what most angers a person can help him to understand himself and his anger. Looking at why that person, situation or action makes him angry may be a starting point to managing anger.

Summary:

Summarize the activity with the following open-ended questions:

— *Do we all get angry?*
— *Do we have the same reasons for getting angry?*
— *Why is it helpful to categorize the reasons that make us angry?*

What Lit My Fuse?
Presentation and Worksheet

Objectives:

— To review and reflect upon the basic concepts of anger: the degrees to which we feel angry, how we respond, and the perceived causes.
— To explore the underlying issues and fears.

Directions:

Note: This worksheet is best used as a culmination to this section, Understanding Anger, as it brings together the elements of how we respond when we are angry, the degrees of anger we feel, and what we perceive to be the causes of our anger. In addition, it moves one step further by exploring the underlying issues of anger. It is geared toward upper elementary students, but primary students could use it as a guided practice.

1. Before distributing the worksheet "What Lit My Fuse?" give a short presentation to the children on the underlying issues related to anger. Say to the group: "We have talked about how our bodies look and feel when we are angry, discussed the degrees of being angry, and investigated some of the causes of anger. Today I want you to think about the issues that lie beneath your anger. The issues have to do with fear. If we really think about what causes our anger, there is usually some fear lurking in the shadows."

Explain that the fears fall into four general categories:

1. Fear of the loss of power
2. Fear of injustice
3. Fear of not being unique or special
4. Fear of not being capable

Say, "Fear of the loss of power is felt when things just don't go our way. We feel helpless. We want to be in control. An example might be when I want to watch my favorite TV program, but dad takes the remote and says he's going to relax after a long workday and watch the football game. You perceive that dad made you mad, but you really feel a loss of power over a situation.

"Anyone can become angry – but to be angry with the right person at the right time, and for the right purpose and in the right way – that is not within everyone's power and this is not easy."

Aristotle

"Fear of injustice happens when we feel that life is unfair, that something is not right or someone is treating you unfairly. You may decide that you wouldn't do what someone else is doing or that they are hurtful and mean. This fear may surface when your teacher makes the whole class stay in during five minutes of recess because a few students were talking when she said to be quiet.

"Fear of not being unique or special has to do with thoughts that arise like 'They must think I'm a jerk,' or 'No one notices me' or 'What kind of person am I anyway?' This could occur when you spill chocolate milk down the front of your shirt or when another person was chosen to be team captain.

"Fear of not being capable happens when you don't think that you can do something, or you feel like you can't do it well enough, like playing baseball or soccer or writing a story. Things just seem too difficult and you don't want to even attempt it, so you get angry."

2. Distribute the worksheet and explain to the students that the task is to think about a time they got angry. Ask them to remember what their bodies told them, what degree of anger they felt, how they reacted, what they think caused the anger, and what the underlying fear or fears might have been. Say that doing this worksheet is a way to practice understanding the real issues that create anger in their lives. Knowing what these fears are can help us face them, lessen their power over us, and perhaps even eliminate some.

3. This worksheet can be done as a homework task, or one the students have several days to complete and reflect upon. When completed, volunteers may share their reflections. It should be optional, however, so that the privacy of those not wishing to share is preserved.

What Lit My Fuse?
Worksheet

Think of a time when you got mad. Something exploded inside of you. Explore this situation by answering the following questions:

1. What was the situation when I got angry? (Don't use any names.) Here is my description of the event:

2. How mad was I? Just a little annoyed, slightly irritated, or was I really ticked-off, furious, enraged? This is the degree to which my anger reached (use one of the anger words to describe the feeling):

3. How did my body feel? Did my face turn red? Did I get a knot in my stomach? Did I clench my fists? Did I shout, or shut down and become silent? Here's what my body did:

4. Who or what did I think made me mad? This is what I thought was the cause of my anger:

5. What could the underlying issue be? Here's what my fear might have been:

Section 2

Expressing Anger

If we keep anger tucked inside, it can have ill effects. We can get sick, moody or even suffer from depression. This segment explores healthy and safe ways of expressing anger, including movement, assertive "I" messages, and art. The purpose of this section is to let children know some appropriate expressions of anger and let them practice them, so that they will remember that they have choices when they are really angry.

Sharing Circle:
A Way That I Express Anger

Sharing Circle:
I Expressed My Anger in a Healthy Way

Expressing Anger Through Movement:
Movin' and Groovin'

Presentation and Puppet Play
The "I's" Have It

Art Activity:
I Get the Picture

Role-Play:
Reversing My Point of View

Worksheet:
The Ripple Effect, a Story-Map

A Way That I Express Anger
Sharing Circle

Objectives:

— To learn that everyone has some way of expressing anger. Some expressions are appropriate, and others are not.

Directions:

Gather the students into a circle and introduce or review the ground rules (see: How to Use This Book — Sharing Circles, page 6).

"When angry, count to four, when very angry, swear."

Mark Twain

Introduce the Topic: "Today we are going to share about how we express our anger. The topic is 'A Way That I Express Anger.' "

Elaborate: "We all need to express ourselves when we get angry, and we do it in a variety of ways. How do you express your anger? Do you yell and scream, jump up and down, hum to yourself, or stomp off to your room or another place? Do you often lose your cool and say things you are sorry for later? Maybe you cry to express your anger. Or draw a picture. Or run around the house or playground. Is your expression of anger acceptable to your family, teachers and friends? How do you feel about the way you express your anger? Take a short quiet time to think about what you do when you get angry. The topic is 'A Way That I Express Anger.' "

Begin the Sharing: Invite the children to take turns speaking. If they are self-conscious about beginning, you can start the sharing. Remember that anyone can pass on sharing, and that each child gets only one turn during this time.

Optional: Conduct a review, if you have time and feel it would benefit the children to hear others repeat what they have shared. This reinforces active listening skills.

Summary:

After each child has had an opportunity to share, ask these thinking questions:

— *What are some ways of expressing anger that seem appropriate to you? Inappropriate?*
— *Why do you think it is important for us to express our anger?*

I Expressed My Anger in a Healthy Way
Sharing Circle

Objectives:

— To become aware of the healthy ways in which we express anger.
— To explore the consequences of expressing anger in a healthy, non-harmful way.
— To learn that we have choices as to how we express our anger.

Directions:

Ask the children to form a circle with chairs so that everyone can see everyone else. Go over the ground rules, inviting each student to volunteer one of the rules she or he remembers until all rules have been stated. Say any that may have been forgotten or overlooked.

Introduce the Topic: "This topic is about how we express our anger in a healthy, non-harmful way. The topic is 'I Expressed My Anger in a Healthy Way.'"

Elaborate: "There are many ways to express anger, and some of the ways are healthy. When we can express anger so that no one gets hurt, including ourselves, and no property is damaged, we don't have to feel bad about getting our 'mads' out. Think of a time when you got mad at someone, or at a situation, and you expressed that anger in a healthy way. Perhaps you went for a long walk or run or you stopped and counted to 10.   Maybe you went to your room and cried. Perhaps you went to a friend or an adult you trust and talked about your anger. It may have been a time when you wanted to throw something or hit someone and you just decided to walk away from the situation and give yourself some time to cool down. You may have written about your anger in a diary or journal or drawn a picture showing how you were feeling. Remember the situation and how you handled it so that no harm was done. When you are ready to share, don't use any names, just talk about the situation and how you chose to express your anger.   Let's take a moment to think quietly. The topic is "I Expressed My Anger in a Healthy Way.'"

"Wise anger is like fire from a flint: There is great ado to get it out; and when it does come, it is out again immediately."

M. Henry

Begin the Sharing: When everyone has shown that they are ready to begin, ask if anyone wants to start the sharing. If the children are timid about being first, go ahead and start by sharing your story. That may put the children more at ease about sharing.   It is OK if anyone wants to pass instead of share.

Optional: If you would like the children to show how well they have listened to each other, ask if anyone can repeat what he or she has heard another person share, without any put-downs or adding anything else to the story. This helps to validate each person's unique experience.

 Summary:

After each person who wants to share has done so, ask these open-ended questions to support the objectives of the activity:

— *What are some of the healthy ways of expressing anger mentioned in the sharing?*
— *How did we feel after we expressed our anger without harming anyone or anything?*
— *Why is it better for everyone when we choose to express our anger in a healthy way instead of a harmful way?*
— *What can we do to remind ourselves that we can choose how we express our anger?*

Additional Topics: To extend the learning you may wish to add these topics for discussion, "A Time I Expressed My Anger In A Hurtful Way," and "A Way In Which I Would Like To Express My Anger."

Movin' and Groovin'
Expressing Anger Through Movement

"Anger is a great force. If you control it, it can be transmuted into a power which can move the whole world."

Sri Swami Sivananda

Objectives:

— To learn acceptable outlets to express anger through movement.

— To practice movements that can be used to express anger.

Materials Needed:

Tape recorder or CD player, tapes or CDs with upbeat music.

Directions:

1. Gather the group in a large room or outdoors and say, "Sometimes we feel so angry that we will explode. We are loaded with energy that needs to get out and express itself. We cannot think to sort out the problem and may even feel out of control. In times like these, it is best to get our bodies moving. If you are playing in a sport, this is a good time to put that angry energy into extra practice. Need practice batting balls? Find a friend to pitch some to you in a park. Or passing the soccer ball? Again a friend and a large field are great. This is a good time to practice shooting baskets, especially if a friend is not available or you don't want to be around anyone. Another way is to dance to some upbeat music, letting your arms punch the air around you. You can also jog or run to the beat of the music"

2. Tell the students that you are going to put on some music so they can get the "feel" of what their bodies would like to do. Ask them to remember a time when they were very mad. Put on the music and invite them to jump, jog, dance, punch the air or do any movement that does not harm another person. Suggest that they continue the activity until they are tired and want to rest.

4. Repeat the lesson with other suggestions of expressing anger through movement. Resistance activities such as pushing against a wall, door frame or willing adult, pounding pegs in a pegboard or pounding a pillow are alternatives. Model these behaviors and let the students practice them. You can offer other suggestions to appropriately express the energy that builds in us: riding a bike, skateboarding, screaming into a pillow, rollerblading, swimming, crying (with a sympathetic other is best) or writing a letter or in a journal. These are not only healthy ways to express anger, but they are good ways to release anger as well.

Summary:

Debrief the students by asking them how they felt before and after, the activity. Ask them if moving their bodies helped them express their anger.

Note: You may also want to use a videotape of aerobic exercise, such as kick-boxing, martial arts or step aerobics, with the children.

The "I's" Have It
Presentation and Puppet Play

*"The strong man is
the man who can
stand up for his rights
and not hit back."*

*Dr. Martin Luther
King Jr.*

Objectives:

— To develop a four-step assertiveness strategy.
— To practice using "I" messages as an alternative to striking back in anger.
— To understand that there is a safe and effective way to express anger verbally.

Materials needed:

Copies of the finger puppet and stick puppet patterns at the end of this activity, scissors, colored markers or crayons, tongue depressors or Popsicle sticks for each student, puppet stage or other background (optional).

Note: Give the children copies of the blank puppet cutouts and have them draw, color and cut out their own puppet characters. These will be used later in the student-practice part of the activity.

Directions:

1. **Introduce the activity.** Tell the children that today they are going to use puppets to practice a way to express anger in which no one is hurt or threatened. Explain that you will show them a way to tell another person how you feel about something they did that made you angry. This time, however, you are not going to use blaming statements, put-downs, or name-calling, like "You always make me drop the ball!" or "You clumsy jerk, you ruined my new shoes when you stepped on them!" or "Why don't you get a clue and notice that it's my turn?" There is a safer, more appropriate way to stand up for yourself and tell the other person how you feel. It's called an "I" message.

2. **Give the Presentation:** "An 'I' message starts with saying 'I,' not 'You.' We are going to learn a four-part 'I' message today to help you express your anger towards another person without them becoming angry in return or feeling threatened by your anger. Here are the steps:

   A. **Say the person's name.** Make sure you face them, look them in the eye, and keep your hands and feet to yourself. This acknowledges them and gets their attention. It is a show of respect.

B. **Next, say 'I feel ...' and use a word to describe how you feel**: angry, irritated, annoyed, frustrated, etc. This honestly and clearly communicates your feeling to the other person so there is no doubt.

C. **Then state the reason you feel that way.** Tell them the cause of your anger, what the problem was for you. This focuses on the problem that created your angry feelings, not the person.

D. **Finally, tell the other person what you want them to do.** This allows the other person to take responsibility for his or her actions without getting angry in return or being embarrassed.

"Pretend you are at home watching TV and your brother comes in and sits right in front of you, blocking your view of the screen. Instead of saying a blaming statement or put-down, use the formula for the 'I' message. For example, you might get up and face your brother (not too close, however) and say, 'Brian, I feel so frustrated when you sit right in front of me, blocking the TV screen. I would like you to move a little to the right or left. Then we both can see.'

"Another example might be on the playground at school. You are bouncing the ball and a friend comes along and grabs it. You could tell them, 'Darnell, I feel mad when you take the ball from me. Please ask me if you can play with it.'

"I'll give one more scenario. This time I'll model it with two puppets. (Put one puppet on each hand, facing each other.) You and your friends are playing kickball. It's your turn to kick, and one of your friends (left-hand puppet moves) says, 'Here comes Peanut Brittle!' You are very embarrassed and give him your 'I' message (moving the right-hand puppet), 'Arturo, I feel embarrassed and angry when you call me that name. Call me by my real name, Brittany.' "

3. **Divide the group into pairs.** Give each person a stick puppet, or ask them to use the ones they have designed themselves. Suggest that they take turns letting their puppet act out the one giving the "I" message in a scenario. Ask them to think of a time they have been angry and wished that they would have used the four-step "I" message to convey

their feelings to another person. Let the children take turns. When everyone has taken a turn, volunteers can have their puppets perform for the whole group in a puppet theater or behind a box or table.

4. **For additional practice:** Invite the children to use finger puppets on the index finger of each hand so they can perform "I" message scenarios for their partners.

Summary:

Summarize the activity by asking the students the following questions:

— *Why is using an "I" message a more appropriate way to express their feelings than blaming or threatening?*
— *In what ways would using an "I" message make you feel more in control of an irritating situation?*
— *Why is it important to practice using "I" messages?*
— *How does using an "I" message show respect for both yourself and the other person?*

I Get the Picture
Art Activity

Objectives:

— To understand that art can be a satisfying expression of anger.
— To experience art as an appropriate expression of anger.

Materials Needed:

Magazines, glue, art paper, colored markers, colored pencils, crayons. Optional: CD or tape player, CDs or audio tapes of music that would express feelings of anger, such as any "heavy metal" or "acid rock" music or any dramatic classical music such as "Mars" from "The Planets" by Gustav Holst.

Directions:

"Depression is rage spread thin."

Paul Tillich

1. Hold a brief discussion of what the students think would happen if we kept our anger inside and didn't express it at all. The answers may vary but should lean toward the idea that trying to keep our anger shut up inside of us will affect our health. It also might come out in other ways, like feeling negative and grouchy all the time. Add the fact that it could lead to a condition called depression, where you feel low energy and sad most of the time. Say to the students that one way to express anger is through art.

2. Distribute the art supplies and magazines. Invite the children to express some anger that they have or have recently had by creating a piece of art that expresses their feelings. They might want to use the markers, pencils or crayons to create a background first. Then they can choose pictures or parts of pictures to glue on top of the background to express their mood. Explain that their art does not have to be a picture of a person or even a thing. It can be parts of pictures that have certain shapes or colors that represent angry feelings. Perhaps something in a picture might be a symbol of what their bodies are feeling inside, like an explosion, a storm or a volcano. You may want to play some music on a CD player or tape player that would fit an angry mood while the children are crafting their art (see: Materials Needed, above).

3. Allow the children ample time to complete the project (20 to 30 minutes). As they are working, you can walk around and ask students to tell you about the feelings they are trying to express in their artwork. Ask if they have a story they want to tell you to go with the artwork.

4. When the project is complete, invite volunteers to share. Post their artworks on a bulletin board and give them titles like "Angry Art" or "Storms, Explosions and Volcanoes ... Our Mad Work."

Summary:

To integrate what has been learned in this activity, ask the students some open-ended questions, such as these:

— *How did it feel to use art to express your anger?*
— *Did the art look like angry art? Why or why not?*
— *How could using art help you to express anger?*

Reversing My Point of View
Role Play

"Consider, when you are enraged at anyone, what you would probably think if he should die during the dispute."

William Shenstone

Objectives:

— To see the point of view of an adversary by placing ourselves in her or his role.
— To appreciate alternative perspectives and behaviors.
— To dissolve, dilute or dissipate our anger by understanding the other side of the conflict.

Materials Needed:

Two chairs for each student.

Directions:

1. Explain to the students that when we are angry with another person, we often only see our own point of view. However, by putting ourselves in the other person's place and looking at the situation from his or her perspective, we can begin to appreciate and understand that person's motivations, feelings and behaviors. This broadened point of view will dilute, dissolve or dissipate our anger. Tell the students that one way to do this is to sit in a chair facing another, empty chair in which you imagine the person you are angry at is sitting. Then you can talk to the person from your point of view, using "I" messages. When you have said all that you need to say, you change chairs and pretend you are the other person, talking from what you imagine to be her or his point of view.

2. Have the children each take two chairs and place them so they face each other.   Invite them to sit in one of the chairs and ask them to remember a time when they were angry at someone. Perhaps they are angry at someone now. Ask them to imagine that the other person is sitting in the chair facing them.

3. Tell the children that their task is to talk to the person in the empty chair, telling them the things that he or she did to upset them or make them angry. Suggest that they use "I" messages or any other form of communication that will effectively express their feelings. Give the children two to five minutes to do this part of the activity.

4. Next, ask the children to switch chairs and imagine that they are the other person. For example, if they are angry at a friend, they will pretend that they are the friend and speak from that person's point of view. They will respond to what they had said in the first part of the activity. Give the children two to five more minutes to accomplish this part of the task.

5. Finally, ask the children to switch back to the original chairs, becoming themselves again. They may say what they need to in response to the "other" person again. The activity can continue back and forth as long as the person still feels angry and has not come to appreciate the other point of view.

6. While the students are doing both parts of the activity, circulate around the group and coach the children to really "confront" their invisible partner, playing both roles as they switch chairs.

7. Debrief the students and summarize the activity with the following questions:
    — *How did it feel to take both sides in a confrontation?*
    — *Did it help you clarify your own point of view by taking the role of the other person for a while? How?*
    — *Did it help you understand the other person's point of view by pretending that you were that person and responding to your original communication? How?*
    — *How can you benefit from this activity when you are away from school?*

Note: You can do a variation of this activity by having the students imagine a particular worry, gripe or grudge sitting in the empty chair. They can imagine that the worry, gripe or grudge has the physical features of a friendly creature. Instruct them to have a conversation with the creature; then switch chairs to become the worry, gripe or grudge. Encourage the students to ask the creature questions that they will try to answer when they play the role of the creature. Follow the activity with similar discussion questions as those above.

Story-Mapping the Ripple Effect
Literature and Worksheet

Objective:

— To develop an understanding of the far-reaching consequences of inappropriate expressions of anger.

Materials Needed:

A copy or multiple copies of "Andrew's Angry Words" by Dorothea Lachner, North South Books (1995), a copy of the worksheet "The Ripple Effect Story-Map," colored pencils, fine-tip markers or crayons.

Directions:

1. Introduce the activity by explaining that the consequences of what we say are far-reaching and can spread from person to person. Ask the students, "Have you ever had someone say something nice about you, making you feel good for a long while after that? Perhaps you, in turn, were nice to someone else who was kind to yet another person." Continue the discussion with another question, "How would you feel if someone called you a bad word or swore at you?" Answers may include that it makes us feel mad, sad or hurt.

2. Tell the group you are going to read a book to them about a boy named Andrew who uses angry words when his sister trips over him, and they are passed on from one person to another. It is like the ripple effect a stone makes when you throw it into water. The ripples keep extending outward. Explain that the book is a cautionary tale, like a fable — one that teaches a lesson.

3. Read "Andrew's Angry Words" to the group or have them divide into small groups and do a "read-around" in which each student reads a page, shows the picture and passes the book to the next person until the book is finished. The story begins when Andrew's sister trips over him and he uses swear words to express his anger. The words are passed on from person to beast to person. Finally, the words cause complete chaos until they reach a wise old woman, who refuses to use them. Instead, she tucks them into a bag, which she tosses into the sea. She replaces them with kind and happy words, which she gives to Andrew to take home. The story then reverses itself with the bundle of kind words.

"Anger is as a stone cast into a wasp's nest."

Unknown

4. After reading the story, distribute the worksheet, "The Ripple Effect, A Story-Map." Ask the students to list the events of the story in order. You may write these on the chalkboard or whiteboard or have the students list them on the back of their worksheets. Say that they will make a story map of the events by drawing a picture of each event in the empty squares, starting at the top.

Summary:

Debrief the students by asking:

— *What happens when anger gets out of control?*
— *Has the "ripple effect" ever happened to you?*
— *Why do you think it is important to not use swear words, put-downs, sarcasm or criticism when you are angry?*

The Ripple Effect, A Story Map
Student Experience Sheet

Start Here

1

2

3

Create a story map of the events that happened in the story "Andrew's Angry Words." Draw a picture of each event in the empty squares. Put the events in order beginning with number one.

5

4

6

7

8

End Here

Controlling Anger

There are times when it is prudent to keep our anger under control. We may be in a public setting or in a place in which there is no opportunity to express it in safe and acceptable ways. If we don't keep it under control, we may say something that we regret or do something that will hurt someone. In this section, children will learn a variety of effective and satisfying ways to control anger and learn how to help others calm their own anger as well. The children will practice and review these strategies so that their positive responses become automatic at times of heightened emotions.

Sharing Circle:
I Was Angry and Kept It Under Control

Sharing Circle:
A Time I Lost Control and Regretted It

Positive Statements for Self-Talk:
Change Your Thoughts

Relaxation Strategies:
Get a Handle on Your "Mads"

Strategies to Help Others Control Their Anger:
You Must Be Really Mad!

Creating a Song Worksheet:
There's Music in the Air

I Was Angry and Kept It Under Control
Sharing Circle

Objectives:

— To aware of when anger must be controlled
— To acknowledge ourselves for keeping our anger under control.
— To share the different ways we have learned to control anger.

Directions:

Call a group of children to form a circle. State or review the ground rules for the circle (see: How to Use This Book — Sharing Circles, page 6).

Introduce the Topic: Say, "Our topic for this Sharing Circle is 'I Was Angry and Kept It Under Control.'"

Elaborate: "Anger is one of the most difficult emotions to manage. It doesn't feel good and it's sometimes hard to control. In this session, we are going talk about a time when we successfully controlled our anger. Think of a time when you were angry at someone or at a situation, but you did something to control yourself. Maybe you slowly counted to 10, bit your lip, folded your hands or did something else to keep from blowing up. You may have been mad at a brother or sister, a parent, friend or teacher, and it could have been over something important or just a small thing. Tell us what happened and how you controlled your anger. Please don't mention any names. Think quietly about it for a few seconds before we begin. The topic is 'I Was Angry and Kept It Under Control.'"

Begin the Sharing: Let anyone who wants to start do so. If there is reluctance on everybody's part to begin, you may want to break the ice by sharing. Keep in mind that everyone gets an equal amount of time, but anyone can choose not to share.

Optional: If you feel that the children would benefit by practicing active listening skills, conduct a review by asking if anyone remembers what another group member has said. Let the children hear from others what they have shared. It helps to acknowledge what they shared.

Summary:

When the sharing is complete, conduct a summary by asking some open-ended questions:

— *Do you think it is beneficial to control our anger? Why or why not?*
— *What are some ways in which we can control our anger?*

"If you are patient in one moment of anger, you will escape a hundred days of sorrow."

Chinese proverb

A Time I Lost Control and Regretted It
Sharing Circle

Objectives:

— To understand the consequences of losing control of our anger.

— To realize that we have choices as to what we say and do when we are angry.

— To learn that it is more beneficial for all concerned when we keep our anger under control.

Directions:

Form a circle of chairs and invite the students to take seats facing each other. Review the ground rules of the Sharing Circle. You may ask the children to each volunteer one of the rules until all are covered. Fill in any that were overlooked.

Introduce the Topic: "This Sharing Circle will be 'A Time I Lost Control and Regretted It.'

Elaborate: "This time we are going to share about a time in which we lost control of our anger and were sorry for it afterwards. Lots of things make us angry, but sometimes when we are already feeling bad about something else or we are hungry, tired or sick, we may lose control. We will do or say something that we later regret. We have all done it at one time or another: shouted at someone, called someone a bad name or threw something and broke it. Losing control doesn't mean that we don't get angry. It means that we do something we would not normally do to ourselves, to another person or to a piece of property. We wouldn't normally yell at a baby sister, but if we let our anger get away from us, we may scream at her and make her cry. That makes us feel even worse. Have you ever picked up something of your own or someone else's and broke it deliberately in anger? How did you feel after you broke it? Did you ever kick someone and hurt that person badly because you were so full of rage? Did you feel sorry after you did it? Is there something that you did in anger that you still regret after a long time has passed? When you are ready to share, remember to not use any names. Talk about the situation, how you lost control, and how you felt about it then and now. Let's sit silently for a moment to think about 'A Time I Lost Control and Regretted It.' "

"Indulge not thyself in the passion of anger; it is whetting a sword to wound thine own breast, or murder thy friend."

Akhenaton

Begin the Sharing: When everyone has had a quiet moment to think about the topic, you can invite anyone to share who wishes to. Sometimes it takes a minute or so for the first volunteer to start, so allow that safe space for someone to chime in. If no one begins sharing, it may be a good idea to begin yourself. This may encourage others to follow. Remember that anyone can pass on it.

Optional: When the sharing is complete, you may want to ask the children to remember what another person in the circle has shared. This is an opportunity for the children to restate what they heard. This helps them to acknowledge and validate the importance of what each person has said. It also reminds the group of what they can learn from the sharing before you discuss it in the Summary.

 Summary:

After the sharing, lead a summary by asking the following open-ended questions:

— *What are some of the ways in which we lost control of our anger?*
— *Why do you think we lose control of our anger sometimes?*
— *How does "losing it" make us feel after we have done so?*
— *How does "losing it" make us feel much later?*
— *What are the signs that we are on the verge of losing control?*
— *What are some choices we can make to avoid losing control?*

Additional Topic: Another topic to use is "A Good Way I Control My Anger." This helps the students focus on solutions to problems anger can create.

Change Your Thoughts
Positive Statements for Self-Talk

"The one who cannot restrain their anger will wish undone what their temper and irritation prompted them to do."

Horace

Objectives:

— To develop an understanding that thoughts precede feelings.
— To change negative attitudes by using positive self-talk.

Materials:

Paper, pencils, 3-by-5-inch cards.

Directions:

1. Introduce the activity by talking about how thoughts precede feelings. Say, "In any given situation, we will have an instantaneous thought about it and the feeling will follow. This is called self-talk. It is like having a conversation with yourself, which is what your mind does all the time. For example, you are carrying your lunch tray to a table when your shoe comes off and you trip, sending your lunch all over the floor. Your immediate thought is, 'I am really clumsy.' The feelings that follow it will probably be anger and embarrassment.

   "One way to change or prevent the angry feelings from emerging in any given situation is to change the thoughts. You can do this by creating positive statements to tell yourself. They can be about how you do something, like 'I can learn my multiplication facts easily and quickly.' Positive statements can be ones that tell you to react differently in a situation than you usually do. 'I am calm and confident when I try to swim across the pool.' You can use positive statements to change your belief about something. For example, if you feel you have no friends, you could use a statement like 'I am a good friend' or 'I attract lots of friends to myself.'"

2. Give the rules for making positive statements:
   The statement must be stated in the positive. You can't use "no," "never" or "not."
   The statement must be stated in the present tense. Do not use the past or future tenses.
   Say the statement as if it were true. This helps to "change" those negative thoughts that your mind is used to thinking.

3. Some suggestions of positive thoughts that you can share with the children are:

> I stay calm when someone calls me a silly name.
> I am a happy person at all times.
> I ignore my little sister when she bothers me.
> I am a good student.
> I control my temper on the football field.
> I am a strong, fast runner.

4. Invite the children to think of annoying or worrisome thoughts that they have about themselves that could trigger anger. Give them time to identify what they are and to write them in a list on paper. Ask them to choose the one or two they most want to change. Then suggest that they reverse the thought and make it a positive statement. Distribute one or two 3-by-5-inch cards to each student. Have the students write their reversed statements on the cards in large, bold print and carry the cards with them for the next month. Suggest that they create only one or two positive statements at a time to focus on and practice. They will have "changed" their minds when they automatically think those positive thoughts. Collect the negative statement papers and dramatically rip them up and throw them into the trash.

5. Brainstorm with the group to decide where and when they will practice and use their positive statements. It may be when they get up in the morning, when they go to bed at night, every time they pass a mirror, at recess, before or after each meal, or once every hour. After getting suggestions, each child can decide for her- or himself when, where and how often she or he will practice the statements during the next month. Ask each of the students to write that down on the reverse side of the positive statement card. Tell them that the more they say their statements, the quicker their minds will adjust to believing the statements.

▮ Summary:

After a month of "coaching" the students to use self-talk with positive statements, ask them to share their experiences. Ask if anyone's mind has changed about something as a result of repeating the statement. Invite students to share about changes in behaviors and feelings related to the positive statements being repeated. If the experience has been positive, work on one or two more statements for the next month.

Get a Handle on Your "Mads"
Relaxation Strategies

"Anger is a momentary madness, so control your passion or it will control you."

Horace

Objectives:

— To learn strategies for controlling anger.
— To implement behavioral techniques for controlling anger.

Directions:

1. **Introduce the activity.** Begin by reviewing with your students the idea that getting angry is a reaction that comes naturally. Say, "We all get angry and need to learn acceptable and effective ways to deal with it. There are strategies to express anger in appropriate and satisfying ways (See activities in Section 2).

   "What we are going to learn now is how to control yourself when it is not appropriate or convenient to express anger (for example, through strenuous or aerobic physical activity, or some kind of art or craft project). There may be a time during a basketball or soccer game when you have made a foul, in a public place when a sibling has teased you, or during class when everybody is working and you broke your pencil three times trying to finish a story. These are times we need to control anger in quiet ways. I'll show you some ways and then we can practice them together. We will explore five easy ways to control anger quietly: deep breathing, counting, Hook-ups, Positive Points and drinking water."

   Explain the strategies for controlling anger and have the group practice after each explanation.

2. **Belly Breathing:** Explain that belly breathing is taking in breaths slowly and deeply so the stomach is extended. This is an important point. Children tend to extend their chests and think they are taking a deep breath, but the air must push down on the diaphragm, which extends the belly. Next you hold the breath for about two seconds and slowly release the breath. Make sure that all of the breath is out, holding that position for about three or more seconds while relaxing the body. Repeat this five to 10 times. You should notice that the breathing becomes slower and more natural as you go on. It is important that you concentrate on nothing but breathing, listening for the air to enter the lungs. Hold and hear the

exhalation. Hold before repeating the process. If possible, close the eyes while performing the deep breathing. The body and mind should relax, and much of the angry energy should dissipate.

3. **Counting** is something we all can do when we want to keep our cool in a tense or potentially explosive situation. Tell your students to count to 10 very slowly, silently or aloud (depending on the situation). Then count backwards from 10, slowly. Suggest that they concentrate on counting, nothing more. If necessary, they should repeat the process as many times as possible until they feel under control. If they need to count to 25, go ahead. The important thing is to think about the numbers you are counting, drawing your attention away from the angry situation.

4. **Hook-ups** is a position that effectively calms you and helps focus your energy on yourself instead of on the external situation. It can create feelings of safety and peace. Hook-ups is a part of many helpful movements and positions in "Brain Gym," developed by Dr. Paul Dennison of the Educational Kinesiology Foundation. For more information on "Brain Gym," see "How to Use This Book."

    To perform hook-ups, you can stand, sit or lie down. First, you cross one ankle over the other. Then, hold hands in a crossed and inverted position. To do this, hold both arms out straight in front of the body with the backs of the hands facing each other, thumbs pointing toward the floor. Cross one hand over the other and clasp hands as if to shake hands with yourself. Roll the hands downward and into the body, resting them against the chest. While in that position, hold the tip of the tongue against the roof of the mouth. This position connects emotions in the limbic system with reasoning in the frontal lobes of the brain. Hold the position for as long as it takes to calm yourself down (usually a minute or so but maybe longer, depending upon the intensity of the anger). See how long you can stay angry in that position!

5. **Positive Points** is another strategy used in "Brain Gym." Have you ever noticed someone who is under stress touch the forehead above the eyebrows and massage that area? Those are emotional stress release points from "Touch for Health," created by Dr. John Thie and renamed Positive Points by Dr. Paul Dennison. The Positive Points bring blood flow in the brain from the hypothalamus to the frontal lobes, where rational thought occurs, preventing a fight-or-flight response when emotions are high.

   Place the tips of your fingers on the indentations of the forehead a half inch or so above each of the eyebrows. Hold your hands in place for a few minutes, closing your eyes. Notice how you begin to relax and take on a more positive outlook.

6. We often underestimate the importance of keeping the body hydrated. The electrical and chemical actions of the brain and central nervous system are dependent upon how well the electrical currents are conducted between the brain and sensory organs. Water is a key player in this process. When we feel the emotional stress of anger, our bodies become depleted of water, leaving the cells dehydrated. Taking sips of water will rehydrate the cells and allow us to handle our anger better. Any other liquid will be processed like food and cannot substitute for water. Keeping the body hydrated can be a good preventive measure for "losing our cool" during the day.

7. Invite the children to practice these strategies several times in class and at home. Ask them to try them when they are angry and report back on which one worked best for them.

 Summary:

   Anchor the new skills by asking the children to find a partner and share one of the strategies for controlling anger. Take turns "teaching" one another a strategy.

You Must Be Really Mad!
Strategies to Help Others Control Their Anger

Objectives:

— To build a repertoire of phrases in which to help another person calm down.

— To learn to empathize and acknowledge another person's anger.

Materials Needed:

chalkboard and chalk or whiteboard and markers

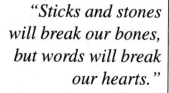

Directions:

1. Introduce the activity by asking the students to remember a time when they were with another person who got angry for some reason. Say, "We all get really uncomfortable when other people lose their cool. If the other person is completely out of control, it is probably best to step away or say nothing until the person calms down a little. If the person becomes violent, leave their presence and get the help of an adult whom you trust. However, there are things you can do and say to a friend or loved one that may help them calm down. We can acknowledge their feelings and show them that we care about them without further fueling their anger."

2. With the students, brainstorm ways they know to acknowledge other people's feelings. Make one or two suggestions to start if they are having trouble thinking of acknowledgements. Ensure that ideas such as the following are included and write them on the board:

    You really look as if you're angry.

    I'm sure you feel badly about that.

    I understand how angry you must be.

    You may be right.

    I am so sorry.

    You sound like you are really hurt/annoyed/frustrated.

    It bothers you a lot, doesn't it?

    You have every right to be furious about that.

    I see that you need to blow off steam.

    Do you want to take some time out to calm down?

    If you'd like to talk about why you are mad, I'll listen.

    Is there anything I can do to help you?

"Sticks and stones will break our bones, but words will break our hearts."

Robert Fulghum

3. Invite volunteers to read the phrases and tell the children that these are examples of caring and calming phrases we can use to help another person calm down when they are angry. Say that they can be used when another person is mad at us or is trying to get us mad. For example, a friend calls you up after school and accuses you of taking his or her homework in school. You know you didn't do it, but you want to show your friend that you care. You may say, "You may be right. Perhaps I picked it up with mine when I was packing away my books. Let me check," or "I hear that you are really mad about this. I didn't take it, but I understand how you feel."

4. Tell the students that they are going to choose a partner and practice some of these caring and calming phrases. After each student has a partner, ask the students to think of a situation that could happen in which someone close to them gets mad. One person could be the person who is angry; the other will try one or more of the caring phrases. Then they will switch roles and act out a different scenario. Have them do this for two or three rounds before gathering the group together to summarize.

 Summary:

Summarize the activity by asking these open-ended questions:

— *How does using one or more of these phrases help to show someone else that we care about them?*
— *How does using these words help to calm another down?*

Listen for answers such as: This helps show that we care by acknowledging the other person's feelings. We don't make the person seem wrong about feeling the way he or she does. We show the person she or he has a right to those feelings. We don't try to take the feelings away. We let the person be angry but don't plug into the anger ourselves.

There's Music in the Air
Creating a song

"The anger of a person who is strong can always bide its time."

John Ruskin

 Objectives:

— To review and anchor the strategies learned to express and control anger.

— To create a song that demonstrates anger-management strategies.

 Materials Needed:

Chalkboard with chalk or whiteboard with markers, one "Music in the Air" worksheet per child, pencils or pens.

 Directions:

1. This activity should be a culmination of this section, "Controlling Anger," and the previous section, "Expressing Anger." Distribute the worksheets to the students and tell them that a good way to remember something new is to put the idea to music. Say that they will create a song telling the ways they have learned to manage anger by controlling or expressing it.

2. Brainstorm with the students strategies on how to control and express anger. List them on the board. Students may suggest some of the following strategies:

   Ride a bike
   Run around the block
   Draw or paint a picture
   Use an "I" message
   Take a slow, deep breath
   Count to 10
   Do Push-ups
   Touch Positive Points
   Drink water
   Use positive statements
   Punch a pillow
   Take time out
   Talk to someone

3. When the students have exhausted their ideas, have them brainstorm simple tunes that they all know, such as "Frere Jacques," "If You're Happy and You Know It," "Mary Had a Little Lamb," "The Noble Duke of York," etc.

4. Divide the children into small groups or pairs. Explain that their task is to create a song demonstrating their knowledge of ways to manage their anger. They can use any known tunes such as the one they brainstormed and put words to them.

Some examples might be:

Using the melody to "Frere Jacques," they could create this song:

"When you're angry, when you're angry,
jog a mile, jog a mile.
You will feel much better, You will feel much better,
Jog awhile, Just a mile."

The tune to "If You're Happy and You Know It" makes an easy song:

"If you're angry and you know it, tell a friend.
If you're angry and you know it, tell a friend.
If you're angry and you know it, you can peacefully
    control it.
If you're angry and you know it, tell a friend."

Here's an example using the melody of "The Noble Duke of York":

"You're mad and fur-i-ous, there are ways to express,
a picture you can draw, or a message using 'I.'
And when you're mad, you're mad, expressing it's not
    bad,
in safe and calming ways, makes happier your days."

5. Ask the children to create as many verses to the songs as they can to show how they can express and control their anger. When the songs are completed, you can suggest that the students add motions.

Note: Upper-graders may want to create a rap instead of a song. They can add sound effects and body motions.

6. After the songs are composed and rehearsed, set aside a time for the students to perform them. Make it a talent show or have them perform the songs during an assembly at school. That will acknowledge their efforts and allow them to demonstrate to others their knowledge of anger management.

There's Music in the Air
Worksheet for Creating a Song

The tune to this song is:

The words to the verses are:

Releasing Anger

Sometimes the best way to manage anger is just to let go of it. It may involve a ritual of releasing, a quiet time alone in meditation, or a choice to forgive another person. Other times, it pays to take the angry energy and channel it positively into changing the situation that caused the anger. This segment ends with a culminating activity to review and analyze appropriate and inappropriate anger-management behaviors.

Sharing Circle:
A Time I Forgave Someone

Sharing Circle:
A Time Someone Forgave Me

Meditation Practices:
Forgiving and Releasing

Ritual for Releasing Anger:
Letting Go of Gripes and Grudges

Creative Visualization:
See It in Your Mind, Create It in Your Life

Using Anger to Create Change:
Take the Anger Challenge

Worksheet:
My Anger Journal

A Time I Forgave Someone
A Sharing Circle

Objectives:

— To understand that we can use the power of love to forgive.
— To acknowledge that we are loving persons.
— To understand that it does not serve us to hold grudges against others.
— To become aware that we can rise above our feelings of anger.

"You cannot shake hands with a clenched fist."

Indira Gandhi

Directions:

Gather the children into a circle and review the Sharing Circle Rules (see: How to Use This Book — Sharing Circle, page6). Ask the students to recite the rules they remember. Contribute those that were overlooked.

Introduce the Topic: "Our topic for this Sharing Circle is 'A Time I Forgave Someone.'"

Elaborate: "Forgiving another person for hurting us or making us angry is not easy. Sometimes we feel that we should get back at the other person, hold a grudge against the person for a long time, or that we have a right to stay angry with them. However, there are times in our lives when we love someone and use that love to forgive the other person. There are other times when perhaps we think about how it would be to be in the other person's shoes, and we begin to feel sorry for them. That may trigger a forgiveness signal in us. Think of a time when you were mad at someone, but decided to forgive the person. Did a brother break one of your toys? Maybe you realized that it was an accident, or that he was mad about being hurt, and you made a choice to forgive him. Perhaps a friend called you an insulting name, but you chose to ignore it and treated her kindly in return. What made you decide to forgive that person? How did you feel after you forgave her or him? Did it affect the other person in any way? Think about a time when you forgave another person. Close your eyes and think about it quietly for a couple of moments before we share. The topic is 'A Time I Forgave Someone.'"

Begin the Sharing: Ask the children, "Would anyone like to begin the sharing?" Wait a minute, if necessary, to give the group members time to think and to summon their courage to share. If no one starts, you may want to share your own story of forgiveness.

Optional: After the sharing is completed, practice active listening by inviting the children to repeat what they heard another person in the group say. Tell them to say, "(Name), I heard you say that..." Invite the other person to say whether she or he felt listened-to and whether the information was accurate.

Summary:

After everyone has had the opportunity to share, lead a summary discussion of the key concepts learned from the Sharing Circle. You may want to ask open-ended questions such as the following:

— *Why might it be better to forgive than not to?*
— *How is forgiving another person different from letting the person hurt us?*
— *How does it feel when we forgive someone?*
— *What makes us decide to forgive another person?*
— *What would it feel like to be the person forgiven?*

A Time Someone Forgave Me
A Sharing Circle

Objectives:

— To acknowledge the people who have forgiven us.
— To appreciate the love and kindness by which we are forgiven.
— To understand how forgiveness heals wounded relationships.

Directions:

Bring the students together into a circle and go over the Sharing Circle rules. Invite them each to remember and restate a rule. Be sure to fill in for any that were forgotten.

Introduce the Topic: Tell the children, "Today, the topic for our Sharing Circle is 'A Time Someone Forgave Me.'"

"To err is human, to forgive divine."

Alexander Pope

Elaborate: "Nobody's perfect, and we all know when we have done something to hurt another person or make them angry. Today we are going to talk about a time when we said or did something that made someone angry or could have made them angry, but instead they forgave us. Think of a time when you did something like drop someone's china figurine or sit on someone's glasses and break them. The other person may or may not have felt angry but let you know that they forgave you. Did you ever say something unkind about a friend, like, 'Oh, he's too slow to be on my baseball team. Let's choose someone else'? Maybe the friend overheard what you said and chose to ignore it and forgave you by remaining your friend anyway. Perhaps you were having a disagreement with a friend and you decided not to speak to her. Later you apologized and said, 'I'm sorry' and she said, 'Not a problem. Let's be friends again.' How did you feel when your friend forgave you? How did the forgiveness affect your relationship? Were you ever mean to someone but they forgave you for hurting them? How did that make you feel? Did you appreciate their act of forgiveness? Please do not use any names, but tell about the circumstances around the act of forgiveness. Talk about how you know the person forgave you, how being forgiven made you feel, and what the forgiveness did to your relationship. Take a minute to think about something that happened to you. The topic is 'A Time I Was Forgiven.'"

Begin the Sharing: After a few moments of quiet thinking time, ask if anyone would like to begin sharing. If no one starts in a minute or so, share your own story first. This may put the students at ease so that they, too, want to share.

Optional: After everyone who wants to share has done so, invite the children to restate what they heard another person in the circle say. This serves as a review so the summary questions can be thoughtfully addressed, and acknowledges everyone's sharing.

 Summary:

When the Sharing Circle is completed, ask these open-ended questions to encourage deep thinking about the lessons learned:

— *What are the ways in which people show us that they forgive us?*
— *How does it feel to have someone forgive you?*
— *How do you feel about the kind of person who forgives you, even if you feel you don't deserve it?*
— *How does forgiveness affect your relationships?*

Additional Topics: You may also choose from these topics on forgiveness: "I Said I Was Sorry, and The Other Person Forgave Me," "A Time I Buried a Grudge," and "A Time We Buried the Hatchet."

Forgiving and Releasing
Meditation Practices

"One of the secrets of a long and fruitful life is to forgive everybody everything every night before you go to bed."

Ann Landers

Objectives:

— To understand what meditation is and what the benefits are.
— To practice meditation in order to release anger and/or forgive another person or situation.

Directions:

1. Give a short presentation on meditation practices covering the basics of what they are and the benefits of meditating. Explain the following: "Meditation is a practice of relaxing and letting go of all thoughts and feelings, except those on which you are focused. It is like a kind of mental martial arts. Meditation can help you to release your anger and forgive. It is best to practice meditation twice a day - in the morning and evening, before a meal is eaten. If you eat first, you may become sleepy during meditation. The best way to do it is to sit in a chair with your eyes closed and to breathe slowly and deeply. It can also be done while walking or standing in place and stretching while you breathe. You can choose a word or a short phrase to focus on, or just listen to your breathing in and out.

Note: Three different meditation practices are described in this activity. Do not attempt to do them all at the same time. Introduce and practice one, allowing the children to practice independently for a couple of weeks or even a couple of months. Then you can introduce another if you think it would be beneficial.

2. **Basic Meditation Practice:** Tell the students to choose a special word, a prayer word or a positive phrase like "thank you." If they want to work on forgiving people, they can use the phrase "I forgive." Some other suggestions are "peace," "shalom," "beauty," "love." As they sit with their eyes closed, they gently let go of any other thoughts, concentrating on the special word, sometimes called a mantra. Take a few deep belly breaths first. On every exhalation, repeat the mantra or phrase. If other thoughts arise, just let them go as if they were balloons floating out of sight.

Let the children practice this for five minutes. Try it each day and add a minute until they reach 10 to 15 minutes. The younger the child, the shorter the time. One minute may be a challenge for some first- and second-graders. If the child is unable to sit still, you can suggest a variation on this. They sit in "Hook-ups" (see: "Get a Handle on Your 'Mads'" in the section "Controlling Anger").

3. **Walking Meditation:** This is similar to the Basic Meditation Practice in that you can choose a mantra, or special word or phrase, and concentrate on it while breathing out. This would be done while walking at an even pace around the block, playground or room, keeping quiet in every other way. Small children will probably find this an easier way to start the practice of meditating. Once again, the focus and intention are important. If the intention is to forgive and release, the children can say, "I forgive" with each outward breath. They can gently let go of other thoughts as they enter the mind. While you have children practice this, you may begin by walking quietly by their sides, eventually letting them walk by themselves.

4. **Stretching Meditation:** This can be done standing or sitting. Stretching the body helps to relax the mind as well. Close your eyes, take in a deep breath, and drop your head to the left shoulder as you exhale. Then bring your head back to the center as you breathe in, and over toward the right shoulder on the next outward breath. Do the same gentle dropping of the head toward the chest and toward the back on alternating breaths. Stretch the arms overhead, backs of hands touching while you inhale slowly. Then float the arms out and down, like making a "snow angel," on the outward breath. Yawning and stretching the face (eyebrows up) while breathing in, and relaxing all the muscles when exhaling is a good way to release stress from the face. A Basic Meditation Practice could follow.

5. **Summarize with checkpoints.** Each week have the children report on how their meditation is going. Remind them not to be impatient if their minds won't stop thinking. Just gently release the thought, like a balloon. Suggest that they try meditation to help them forgive, and invite them to describe how it went for them.

Letting Go of Gripes and Grudges
Ritual for Releasing Anger

"Do not let the sun go down on your anger."

Ephesians 4:26

Objectives:

— To understand that holding in anger can build up and explode or make us sick.
— To understand and experience that writing down what bothers us helps to release the anger.
— To create a ritual of letting go of daily gripes and grudges.

Materials Needed:

An empty coffee can and lid, or a large jar with a lid; a paper label glued or taped onto the can or jar with the words "Gripes and Grudges" on it; small pieces of note paper; pencils.

Directions:

1. Conduct a review of how our bodies feel when we are angry. Ask the children these questions to stimulate discussion:
   — *How does your body feel when you are angry?*
   — *What happens to your energy level when you are angry?*
   — *What would happen to that feeling if we held on to our anger?*
   — *How would we feel if we kept everything that bothers us inside for a long period of time?*
   — *Have you ever been mad at someone and held a grudge for several days or weeks? How did your stomach feel? Did you feel yourself losing energy?*
   — *How well do you study, play and sleep when you are angry?*

   Explain that holding on to our gripes and grudges makes us lose energy and can make us sick.

2. Show the students the can or jar and read the label "Gripes and Grudges." Ask if anyone can tell the rest of the children what a gripe is. Listen for answers such as "something that bugs us," "whatever makes us angry" or "a complaint about something we don't like." Invite volunteers to explain what a grudge is. The children may answer, "staying mad at someone for a long while," "holding on to angry feelings about another person." Say that we are going to create a ritual for releasing, or getting rid of, the gripes and grudges

by using the can. Explain that a ritual is like a ceremony or formal action. Say, "This will be a ritual for releasing our gripes and grudges every day."

3. During the day, invite the children to write down on paper everything and everybody that irritates or annoys them, a separate piece of paper for each gripe or grudge. Then ask them to put their papers into the can or jar, replacing the lid each time a new piece is added.

4. At the end of the day, ask the children if they would like to get rid of their gripes and grudges or hold on to them. If a child wishes to hold on to something, ask her or him to get the paper and keep it until she or he is ready to let go of that "mad." The rest of the gripes and grudges will be ceremoniously destroyed. You can decide how you want to do this for the strongest effect: Use a paper shredder, throw the papers into an outside Dumpster, or burn the papers outside in a hibachi or other fireproof container. Invite the children to say "goodbye" to their gripes and grudges and be ready to start tomorrow fresh and clean.

Summary:

Review the ritual each day by asking the students the following open-ended questions:

— *How does it feel to let go of what is making you angry?*
— *Compare how you feel when you hold on to anger vs. when you release it.*
— *How does writing down what makes you mad help to release it from your mind?*
— *What happens to your energy level when you hold on to your anger?*

Suggest that this can be done at home with the children's families as well.

See It in Your Mind, Create It in Your Life
Creative Visualization

"Every good thing you do, every good thing you say, every good thought you think, vibrates on and on and never ceases."

Peace Pilgrim

Objectives:

— To understand that we can choose to change our feelings about something.
— To learn how to manage anger through visualization.
— To practice visualization in order to release anger.

Materials Needed:

A tape or CD of soft, soothing music like that of Stephen Halpern, Dean Evanson, Ray Lynch or Carlos Nakai, CD or tape player.

Note: This activity can be repeated as many times as you and your students like. You may find that they will ask you to do this visualization after some particularly stressful time.

Directions:

1. Explain to the students that since we all experience anger, it is helpful to learn as many ways as possible to manage it. Say, "One of the ways to manage our anger is by releasing it through a strategy called creative visualization. It is a positive way to handle anger by accepting it and responding to it in a way that is constructive rather than destructive."

2. Ask the children to get into comfortable positions in their chairs or lying down on a carpet, and tell them to close their eyes. Play soft, soothing music on a tape or CD player in the background, making sure that your voice can be heard clearly over the music. Slowly read the script below, pausing frequently to allow the children adequate time for visualizing.

   "Take in a deep, cleansing breath through your nose. Hold it for a second, and slowly release it." (Pause.) "Take several deep breaths, feeling yourself relax more and more with each outward breath." (Pause.) "Let your feet and legs relax." (Pause.) "Feel the tension leaving your shoulders and arms." (Pause.) "Feel your face relaxing and your eyelids becoming heavy like soft, cool clouds." (Pause.) "Now, let your imagination recall a time when you were angry. It could have been recently or a long time ago." (Pause.) "Just think of a time when you were really mad and upset." (Pause.) "Keep breathing deeply and slowly as you remember that moment." (Pause.) "What do you see?" (Pause.) "Is there an angry face or angry faces?" (Pause.) "What do you hear?" (Pause). "Is someone yelling?" (Pause.) "Or is it quiet?" (Pause.) "What did you say?" (Pause.) "Did you shout something mean to someone?" (Pause.) "What did you do?" (Pause.) "Did you kick or hit someone?" (Pause.) "Did you break something?" (Pause.) "Did you do something that you regretted later on?" (Pause.)

"Now, picture in your mind how you would like to change the situation." (Pause.) "What would you like to say or do that is more peaceful?" (Pause.) "What would you like to do to help get your anger out without hurting yourself or another person?" (Pause.) "Could you take a long walk around the block a few times?" (Pause.) "Could you punch a pillow?" (Pause.) "Maybe you would like to write about it in a journal." (Pause.) "What is the right thing for you to do in this situation?" (Pause.) "Maybe you want to let go of your anger like a helium balloon." (Pause.) "Picture yourself doing the best thing for you in that moment." (Pause.) "Say something positive to yourself, like, 'I can handle this easily,' or 'My anger is under control,' or 'I am just going to let go of my anger.'" (Pause.) "While you are still relaxed, let yourself feel good about your new choice." (Pause.) "Now as you become aware of where you are right now, let those positive feelings fill you with peace and joy." (Pause) "You can do this visualization any time you choose." (Pause) "Notice that your breathing is becoming stronger as you gently come back into the room and open your eyes, feeling really good and peaceful."

3. Ask if any students would like to share what they experienced during the creative visualization. Invite them to tell about the original situation and the newly created one and how their feelings changed.

Summary:

Review the strategy in this activity with the following questions:

— *In what ways can creative visualization help us change our feelings?*
— *In what ways can creative visualization help us manage our anger?*
— *How can creative visualization help us to release our anger?*
— *How can you use creative visualization on your own?*

Take the Anger Challenge
Using Anger to Create Change

"The world needs anger. The world often continues to allow evil because it isn't angry enough."

Bede Jarrett

Objectives:

— To understand that anger may be a signal that our needs are not being met, that we are in danger, that our rights are being violated, or that something is not quite right.

— To use the energy created by anger to take positive action.

Materials Needed:

Newspapers, writing paper, pencils

Directions:

1. Introduce the activity by saying that anger is a signal that tells us something. It may be warning us that we are in danger or that our rights are being violated, or that something going on is not quite right. It may be a signal that tells us that our needs are not being met. For example, a friend may try to coerce you to go to the store and steal something. You feel angry. This may tell you that something is not quite right. Your friend may be stealing things and needs to stop. Another example might be that a company keeps sending trucks to dump garbage in a canyon near your home or school. You sense that this could be dangerous to children who play in the canyon. In these cases, you can use your anger to take action to correct the situation. In the first example, you might start by talking to your friend and explain that you feel it is wrong to steal and that you are concerned about his possible behaviors. If your friend ignores what you say and goes ahead and steals, you might take action to talk to an adult about it. In the second example, your anger might be an incentive to start a letter-writing campaign to the company, the enviornmental agencies in your area, or to the local newspaper.

2. Distribute paper and pencils and ask students to list things that are going on that may cause them worry, anger, or concern. Then divide the students into groups and have them share their lists with each other. Let the group decide on 1 situation which they all feel is dangerous, a violation of rights (their own, senior citizens in the area, children, or certain racial groups), or is an indication that their needs are

not being met. Perhaps it is the lack of fresh fruit in the cafeteria or a pothole in the sidewalk to the school, or a leaky roof in the school. It could be a bully who keeps taking the ball away from different kids on the playground or chases children on their way home afer school.

3. After each group has decided on a situation which causes them anger and concern, ask the group to decide on a list of positive actions into which they can channel their anger. It could be writing letters, scheduling a meeting with a teacher or the principal, approaching someone as a group, planning a phone calling campaign (with adult permission), or making posters and asking shop owners to put them in their windows. Ask the groups to decide which action or actions would probably bring the best change. Then invite the groups to take action.

4. Allow an adequate amount of time for this project to take place, perhaps a few days or weeks. After the groups have taken action on a situation, debrief the activity by asking:
   — *Did it help to channel your anger into positive action? Why or why not?*
   — *Was your anger released as you poured your energy into the project?*
   — *What kind of results did your group have? Why?*

Extension Activity: Students may enjoy reading and researching about famous people who used their anger to fight injustice. They could write reports about people such as Lucretia Mott, Susan B. Anthony, Rachel Carson, Mahatma Gandhi, Martin Luther King, Jr. explaining why these people used non-violent social action fueled by their anger to create positive change.

My Anger Journal
Recording and Reporting Anger

"Every day you get many chances to become angry ... You could accept every one, in which case you'll be angry all the time ... You have to separate what is merely annoying from what is really serious."

Ron and Pat Potter-Efron

Objectives:

— To become aware of the times we become annoyed in one day and how we manage the anger.
— To analyze anger-management behaviors and give reasons why they are appropriate or inappropriate.

Materials Needed:

One copy of "My Anger Journal Worksheet" per child, pencils, large chart paper or butcher paper, colored markers.

Directions:

1. Conduct a review of the strategies learned for managing anger by expressing, controlling or releasing it. Remind the students that they can choose how to manage their anger. They will be observing their own anger over the next 24 hours and recording the situations and their responses. Explain that they will choose four times in the next day (or several days, if needed) when they noticed themselves getting annoyed, irritated, ticked-off, enraged, livid, etc.

2. Distribute the worksheets to the children and ask that the students record the anger-producing situations and their responses. Perhaps they count slowly to 10 or jog around the playground, or write down a complaint and put it into the "Gripes and Grudges" can. Maybe they lose their cool and say something that hurts another person's feelings or hit them. Suggest that they be very honest and record exactly how they responded to the anger. This journal is to be completed on their own.

3. When the journals are filled in, divide the children into small groups. Give each group a piece of butcher paper or chart paper (about 36 inches long) and two colored markers. Have a volunteer divide the paper into two columns, labeled "Appropriate" and "Inappropriate." Each child will read from his or her journal and describe the response to the angry situation. The group will come to consensus on whether the behavior was appropriate or inappropriate anger management and record it under the corresponding column.

4. After the charts are filled in, ask each group to post the charts on the wall around the room. Conduct a "gallery walk" in which each group moves to another group's chart at a signal from the teacher. They have a few minutes to read and agree or disagree with the placement of the responses. If they disagree, they will put a dot next to the part they disagree with. The groups will rotate around to the charts until they return to their own. Conduct a discussion in which groups that disagree with a placement of a response will give reasons why they disagree. The original group must explain why they made the placement.

Summary:

To summarize the activity, ask the children to reflect on why it is important to think about what are appropriate or inappropriate ways to manage their anger. Ask them what they think would happen if they did not learn good strategies to manage anger.

My Anger Journal
Worksheet

Record four times when you were angry during a 24-hour period. First, describe the situation. Then tell how you responded, or managed the anger. Be honest, even if you felt that you lost your cool.

1. **Situation:**

My response:

2. **Situation:**

My response:

3. **Situation:**

My response:

4. **Situation:**

My response:

Literature Connection

Activities that enhance the understanding of children's literature can be both fun and instructional. These activities will assist you in providing a wealth of integrated reading, writing, listening, speaking and art in the classroom to increase the students' understanding of stories and concepts about anger. You will enhance their success when you create a classroom environment that respects the opinions of each student and recognizes the advantage of all students working together to gain the most from a literary experience. Using children's literature helps them identify and problem-solve situations that create anger in kids their age. Use these activities sparingly. Don't try to use them all at once. Students will discover activities that they want to do over and over again. The activities stimulate their imaginations and help them relate to the literature, to themselves and to others in meaningful ways.

Bibliography of Children's Books With Anger Themes

Literature-Based Activities:
"The Dandy Dozen"

Bibliography of Adult Books About Children's Anger

Bibliography of Children's Books With Anger Themes

Primary-Grade Literature

Below you will find a list of primary-level books that work well with the activities following this bibliography. Use these books with upper-graders, as well. They can participate in the comprehension activities at a higher level regardless of the level of the book.

Bang, Molly, *When Sophie Gets Angry — Really, Really Angry* (1999)

Bartel, Phyllis, *The Quarrel.* (1989)

Best, Anthony, *That Makes Me Angry* (1989)

Chevalier, Christa, *Spence and the Mean Old Bear* (1986)

Cole, William, *I'm Mad at You, Poems* (1978)

Coleman, William, *Bernie Smithwick and the Purple Shoestring* (1984)

Couture, Susan Arkin, *Melanie Jane* (1996)

Crary, Elizabeth, *I'm Frustrated — Dealing with Feelings* (1992)

Crary, Elizabeth, *I'm Furious — Dealing with Feelings* (1996)

Crary, Elizabeth, *I'm Mad — Dealing with Feelings* (1992)

Duncan, Riana, *When Emily Woke Up Angry* (1989)

Everitt, Betsy, *Mean Soup* (1992)

Farrington, Liz, *Painting the Fire* (1995)

Hargreaves, Roger, *Mr. Grumpy* (1999)

Hautzig, Deborah, *It's Not Fair* (1986)

Hogan, Paula Z., *Sometimes I Get So Mad* (1980)

Holland, Isabelle, *Henry and Grudge* (1986)

Joosse, Barbara M., *Dinah's Mad, Bad Wishes* (1989)

Keller, Beverly, *Don't Throw Another One, Dover* (1976)

Lachner, Dorothea, *Andrew's Angry Words* (1995)

Marcus, Irene Wineman and Paul, *Scary Night Visitors* (1993)

Marzollo, Jean, Dan and Dave, *Football Friends* (1997)

Mayer, Mercer, *I Was So Mad* (1983)

Moser, Adolph, *Don't Pop Your Cork on Mondays: The Children's Anti-Stress Book* (1988)

Moser, Adolph, *Don't Rant and Rave on Wednesdays* (1994)

Nicklaus, Carol, *Katy Rose Is Mad* (1975)

Oram, Hiawyn, *Angry Arthur* (1997)

Parkinson, Jami, *Amazing Mallika* (1997)

Preston, Edna Mitchell, *The Temper Tantrum Book* (1978)

Riley, Susan, *Angry* (2000)

Schami, Rafik, *Fatima and the Dream Thief* (1996)

Scharmat, Mitchell, *Come Home, Wilma* (1980)

Skocz, Anita Joyce, *Crystal Star Angel* (1994)

Thaut, Pamela, *Spike & Ben* (1991)

Tulloch, Richard, *Danny in the Toybox* (1991)

Viorst, Judith, *Alexander and the Terrible, Horrible, No Good, Very Bad Day* (1972)

Whiteside, Karen, *Brother Mouky and the Falling Sun* (1980)

Winn, Christine M., *Monster Boy* (1996)

Wood, Audrey, *Elbert's Bad Word* (1988)

Upper-Grade Literature

With your upper-graders, you may want to do literature circles lasting one to two weeks to explore a few children's novels that address anger in 9- to 13-year-olds. However, the same comprehension activities that follow this bibliography can be used as with the primary books. You don't have to wait until the end of the book to do many of the activities. They can be done at any time as the book is read.

Cleary, Beverly, *Dear Mr. Henshaw* (1983)

Hopper, Nancy J., *Ape Ears and Beaky* (1984)

DeClements, Barthe, *Tough Loser* (1994)

Pitts, Paul, *Racing the Sun* (1988)

Paterson, Katherine, *Bridge to Terabithia* (1972)

Smith, Robert Kimmel, *The War with Grandpa* (1984)

Slote, Alfred, *The Trading Game* (1990)

The Dandy Dozen
Literature-Based Activities

Children's literature can be a powerful yet delightful tool to teach concepts about anger. Combined with the meaning-making activities that follow, literature can be a door through which your students pass to a greater understanding of themselves and others. The literature activities can act as catalysts to change undesirable thoughts, feelings and behaviors. Choose one as a follow-up activity after you have read one of the primary-level books. (Remember that upper-grade students also love being read to and still enjoy the so-called "easy" books.) Use one or more activities during logical stopping places in upper-grade novels. This will assist the students in reflecting and understanding the dilemmas involving anger that children their own ages face in everyday life.

These strategic activities are listed and described below. The handouts supporting them follow the descriptions. Choose the one or ones that best suits the children's book you are using. You can use any of the books from the "Bibliography of Children's Books With Anger Themes."

1. Sketch to Stretch

Objective:

— To make meaning of a story through visuals.

Materials Needed:

Storybook or children's novel, white art paper, colored markers, pencils or crayons, magazine pictures or anything else to create a graphic.

Directions:

Read a story (or several chapters of a children's novel) to the children or have them read the story in pairs or small groups. Divide the children into small groups and ask them to discuss what most intrigued them in the story. Instruct them to consider the whole text that was read, or a character, episode, symbols or the theme of anger. Allow their interpretation to guide them into creating a visual to share with the class. Invite the children to create a group visual, one in pairs, or as individuals. Ask the students to share and explain how their visuals address the theme of anger in the book.

2. Hot Seat

Objective:

— To increase understanding of a book character's thoughts, feelings and behaviors by taking on the persona of the character.

Materials Needed:

A storybook or children's novel, a special chair designated as the "Hot Seat" for each small group, copies of the "Hot Seat Questions" handout (one per student), pencils. Optional: an overhead projector with a transparency of the "Hot Seat Questions" handout.

Directions:

This is a group activity that allows students to assume the persona of a character in the literature being read. It is best done after reading the whole text or enough of the text so that the personalities of the characters are understood. Choose three or four of the characters from the story and brainstorm with the whole group possible questions they could ask each character. Distribute the "Hot Seat Questions" sheet to the students and have them fill in characters' names and corresponding questions as they are discussed. The questions may focus on why a character became angry or acted as he or she did. Higher-level questions such as, "What would you do if …?" or "Why did you do …?" encourage creativity and imaginative yet appropriate responses. You may also choose to make an overhead transparency of the "Hot Seat Questions" sheet and write the questions for each character on the transparency as the whole group brainstorms them.

Next, divide the class into three to five "expert" groups. Each group will choose one of the characters in the story and share ideas about that character. They can rehearse possible answers to questions that may be asked of the character they are to represent.

Invite one student from each "expert" group to form a small group of three to five students (depending on the number of characters chosen). Spread the groups around the room, each with a special chair labeled "Hot Seat." One at a time, the students (in character) sit in the Hot Seat and answer questions from others in the group in a way that would reflect the persona of that character. Each character is given two to five minutes to answer questions posed by other members of the group. You can use a timer to time each Hot Seat rotation. Continue the process until each character has had an opportunity to be in the Hot Seat.

Note: You can use puppets or character masks as props for the students.

"Let there be peace on earth and let it begin with me."

Sy Miller and Jill Jackson

3. Tableau

Objectives:

— To provide active participation opportunities for the students.
— To draw students into the story so that they can make character explorations and interpretations beyond the text.
— To offer the audience an additional perspective on the story.

Materials Needed:

Storybook or children's novel.

Directions:

After reading the story or a significant event in the story, select a scene from the book or invite the students to select a scene to create in a "frozen" form, called a tableau. Divide the class into groups, enough in each group for the number of characters in the scene plus one or two "directors." Each group decides how they will portray the scene, where they will stand, and what character each will represent. The directors will help the characters position themselves in the tableau. When the characters are in their frozen positions, one of the student directors touches the shoulder of one of the characters to signal him or her to speak. The character says a few sentences expressing his or her thoughts and feelings about the scene of the tableau and then freezes in position again. The director goes around and touches one character at a time until all have had a chance to speak. Each group gets a turn to make a tableau, thus offering the others an additional perspective on the story.

4. Open Mind

Objective:

— To understand what goes on in the mind of a specific literary character.

Materials Needed:

Storybook or children's novel, one copy of the "Open Mind" handout for each student, pencils or fine-tip colored markers.

Directions:

After reading a book or part of a book, ask the students to think about a character and what s/he is thinking at a particular moment in the story. Distribute the "Open Mind" handout to each child in the class. Instruct the students to write the name of the character on the top of the paper. You may assign a character for everyone, or the students can choose the character they want to explore. Inside the outline of the character's head, have the students draw symbols or pictures to illustrate what the character is thinking or feeling, what his or her motivations are, or how the character perceives himself or others. In other words, show what is going on in the character's mind. Students may use pencils or colored markers to show the symbols and pictures. You may want to allow for some words, but they must be short expressions and not sentences. The idea is to use symbology and picture writing to interpret the character's perceptions.

Note: You may want to make an overhead transparency of the "Open Mind" and do one character with the whole group to model the process. You can invite volunteers to come and draw the symbols or pictures right on the overhead transparency.

5. Venn Diagram

Objective:

— To visually organize similarities and differences in stories or characters.

Materials Needed:

One copy of the "Venn Diagram" handout for each student, pencils, storybook or children's novel.

Directions:

This activity can be used to compare two characters from the same or different books, or to compare the general story of two books. For example, you might want to compare the character Elbert from the book "Elbert's Bad Word" by Audrey Wood (1988) with the character Andrew from "Andrew's Angry Words" by Dorothea Lachner (1995). After reading the books, distribute the "Venn Diagram" handout to each child. The diagram consists of two overlapping circles. Ask the children to write the name of a character (in this example, Elbert and Andrew) above each circle. In the outer portions of the circles (where they do not overlap), instruct the students to write, in short phrases or sentences, what is different about each character (or story). In the overlapping part, invite them to write what is similar in the two characters (or stories).

Note: If the students are unfamiliar with the Venn Diagram, make an overhead transparency of the "Venn Diagram" handout and demonstrate this compare-and-contrast activity for them before assigning them one on their own. This activity can also be done in pairs or small groups.

6. Tea Party

Objective:

— To understand the concepts of a story by discussing questions or reciting quotes in pairs.

Materials Needed:

Storybook or children's novel, a list of open-ended questions about a story, or one piece of paper for each student with a quote or passage from the story.

Directions:

Have the open-ended questions prepared in advance or brainstorm the questions with the whole group and write them down on paper. If you use quotes or story passages, you may also want to brainstorm the important ones with the whole group. Students are asked to form two concentric circles or a double line, facing each other. The teacher asks one question at a time and students discuss the answer with the person in front of him/her. After both students have discussed the question, one of the lines (or circles) moves one place to the left (or right). The teacher continues until all of the questions are asked. If you use quotes or passages from the story, give each student a paper with the quote written on it and have him/her recite the quote or passage. One of the lines or circles moves one over after each person has spoken until everyone in a group has had a chance to share with each person in the other group.

7. Double Entry Journal

Objectives:

— To actively involve the students in comprehending the story by encouraging interaction with the text.
— To use reflective questioning to analyze characters' motivations, perceptions and behaviors.

Materials Needed:

Storybook or children's novel, several copies of the handout "Double Entry Journal," pencils.

Directions:

This activity works best with upper-grade students and a children's novel, although you can simplify it to be used with primary students and a storybook. Distribute several copies of the "Double Entry Journal" handout to each child. You may staple the copies together in advance to create a book-like journal for each student. On the left side of the paper, labeled "Quotes," the student copies a quotation or passage from the book that he/she is reading or that the class is reading together. Students are encouraged to find quotations that reveal something enlightening, interesting or stimulating about the story or about one of the characters in the story. On the right side of the paper, labeled "My Thoughts," the students respond to the quotation, making personal connections, evaluations, reflections or interpretations of the quote on the left. This is done repeatedly as the students progress through the reading of the book. Periodically, invite volunteers to share their double entries with the rest of the group.

"Consider when you are enraged at anyone what you would probably think if he should die during the dispute."

William Shenstone

8. Directed Reading-Thinking Activity (DRTA)

Objectives:

— To use prior knowledge, textual and/or visual clues to anticipate the content of a story.
— To monitor comprehension of a story by reading to confirm or reject predictions.

Materials Needed:

Storybook or children's novel. Optional: pencils and writing paper or drawing paper and colored markers, pencils or crayons.

Directions:

This activity involves three steps: predicting, reading and proving. Before you read the book to the children or before they read the book, ask the students to read the title of the book, look at the pictures and make predictions about the story. The students discuss, write (using pencils and writing paper) or draw (using drawing paper and colored pencils, markers or crayons) what they think the story will be about. Divide the story into segments or use chapters as natural dividers. The students proceed through each segment or chapter to check their predictions with you and/or their peers. The students evaluate their predictions, refine them or make new predictions before they read a new segment or chapter. Ask the students to provide proof for their predictions by reading the text for verification or acknowledging their background knowledge. This ongoing process of interaction between the words of the author and the background knowledge of the students focuses their attention on a particular purpose for reading the story.

9. Transformation

Objective:

— To demonstrate understanding of a story by transforming it into a poem, play, song, rap or ABC book.

Materials Needed:

Art paper, colored pencils and pens; or crayons and stapler (for creating an ABC book); writing paper and pencils (for poem, play, song or rap); storybook or children's novel.

Directions:

After the reading of the storybook or children's novel with an anger theme, invite the students to become magicians and transform the story into a poem, play, song, rap or ABC book. Divide the class into pairs or small groups and have each select a genre into which they will change the story while maintaining the main idea and theme of the story.

10. Literary Report Card

Objectives:

— To evaluate the attitudes, behaviors, talents and abilities of a character in a story.
— To determine criteria for evaluating the character.

Materials Needed:

A copy of the handout "Literary Report Card" for each child, two children or small group; pencils, storybook or children's novel.

Directions:

After reading the book, explain to the children that the Literary Report Card will assist them in evaluating various aspects of the main character. The notion of giving grades to characters should be fun and easy, since it is a common experience in each student's life. Use whatever grading system the children are used to: letter grades (A to F); pluses and minuses; or "Excellent," "Satisfactory" or "Needs Improvement." Distribute a copy of the "Literary Report Card" handout to each student, pair or small group. Brainstorm the subjects to be graded, based on the story just read. Character traits such as thoughtfulness, responsibility, anger control, appropriate expression of anger, maturity and friendliness are good subjects for the children to evaluate. Have the students come to an agreement on five subjects for the report card and have them put them in the spaces in the "Subject" column. Then invite the students to work in pairs or small groups to give a grade for each subject. The children must come to a consensus about the grade. Then they write a reason or justification for the grade in the "Comment" column next to each grade. If the children are in pairs, one person can write in the agreed-upon grade and the other can write in the comments. After the grades have been decided and comments written in, invite the students to share their report cards with the whole group.

11. Somebody Wanted But So

Objective:

— To determine the main idea of a story by placing the events in a simple pattern.

Materials Needed:

An overhead projector; an overhead transparency of the handout "Somebody Wanted But So"; one copy of the same handout for each student, pair of students or small group; pencils; storybook or children's novel.

Directions:

Explain that most stories can be looked at in this simple pattern that shows that characters have problems just like we do. Demonstrate with a known story like "Cinderella." Project the transparency of "Somebody Wanted But So" on the overhead projector. Ask the students who the somebody is and write in "Cinderella" in that shape when the answer is given. Next ask what Cinderella wanted and write in "to go to the ball" in the shape labeled "Wanted." Explain that most stories have a problem for the main character to overcome. Ask what Cinderella's problem was and write in "her wicked stepmother and stepsisters wouldn't let her" in the shape labeled "But." A solution to the problem arises in the story and it is written in the shape labeled "So." When a volunteer shares the solution to Cinderella's problem, write "her fairy godmother helped her." The same pattern can be used for another problem in the story, the lost slipper. After reading the anger story or novel, distribute copies of the handout "Somebody Wanted But So" to each student, pair of students or small group. Ask them to fill in the pattern just like the Cinderella example, using the characters and events from the story just finished. For example, if you read "Angry Arthur" by Hiawyn Oram (1997), the pattern would read like this: "Somebody" – "Arthur," "Wanted" – "to stay up and watch a Western on TV," "But" – "his mother said no because it was too late," "So" – "Arthur got angrier and angrier until he created a universe-quake." After the task is completed, ask the students to share their patterns with the whole group.

12. Story Belt

Objective:

— To demonstrate understanding of the sequence of events by creating panels on a belt.
— To retell a story using a story belt.

Materials Needed:

Unlined 3-by-5-inch cards or 3-by-5-inch pieces of chipboard or cardboard (six to nine pieces for each pair or group of students), hole puncher, heavy string, yarn or twine, colored pencils, markers or crayons, writing paper and pencils, storybook or children's novel.

Directions:

After reading the story or novel, divide the children into pairs or small groups. Ask the children to write the important events of the story on a piece of paper and sequence them by writing 1, 2, 3, etc. next to each event. Remind the students to include the problem, any failed attempts at solving the problem, and how the problem was solved. Ask them to decide on five to eight of the most important events for their story belt. Distribute the 3-by-5 cards or pieces of cardboard and crayons, markers or pencils and invite the students to draw a story event on each panel, vertically. Have them save a panel for the title of the book. When the panels have been completed with pictures of the events, punch a hole in each of the four corners. Assemble the belt by lacing the string, yarn or twine in the first top hole and out the next until the last panel is connected. Do the same with the bottom holes, lacing the string in and out. Make sure the belts begin with the title panel and continue with the event panels in order from left to right. Leave a long piece of string hanging on each end of the top and bottom holes. The person the pair or group picks to wear the belt will tie the top and bottom pieces into bowknots in front. That person will revolve, showing the event panels while the other(s) retell the story. The children can take turns wearing the belt and telling the story to another group or pair of students.

Hot Seat Questions
Handout

_____
Name of Book

_____
Name of Character

Questions: _____

_____

_____

_____
Name of Character

Questions: _____

_____

_____

_____
Name of Character

Questions: _____

_____

_____

_____
Name of Character

Questions: _____

_____

_____

Open Mind
Handout

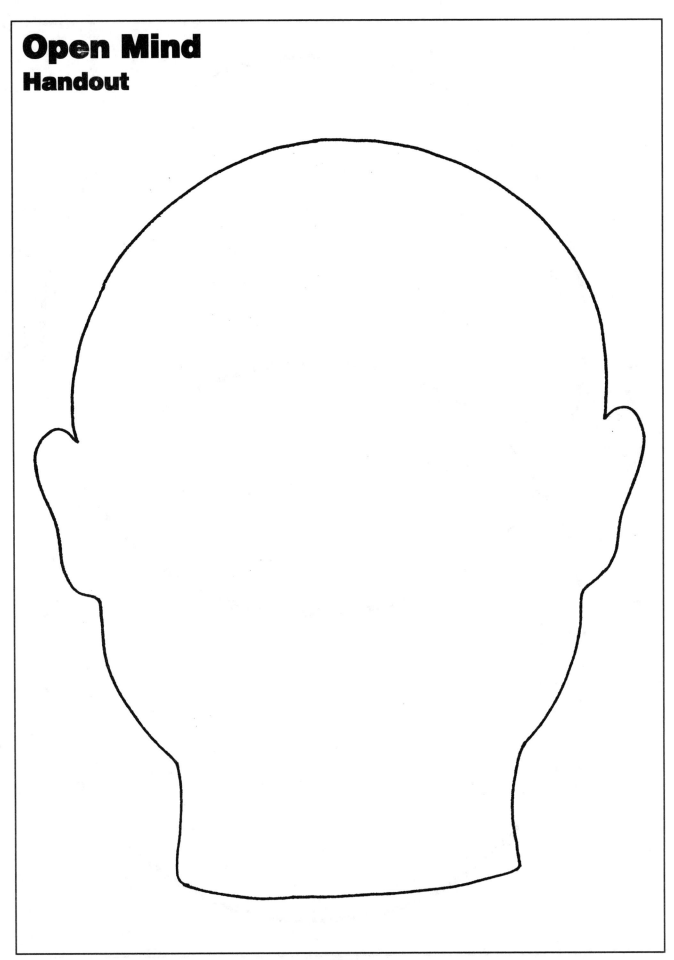

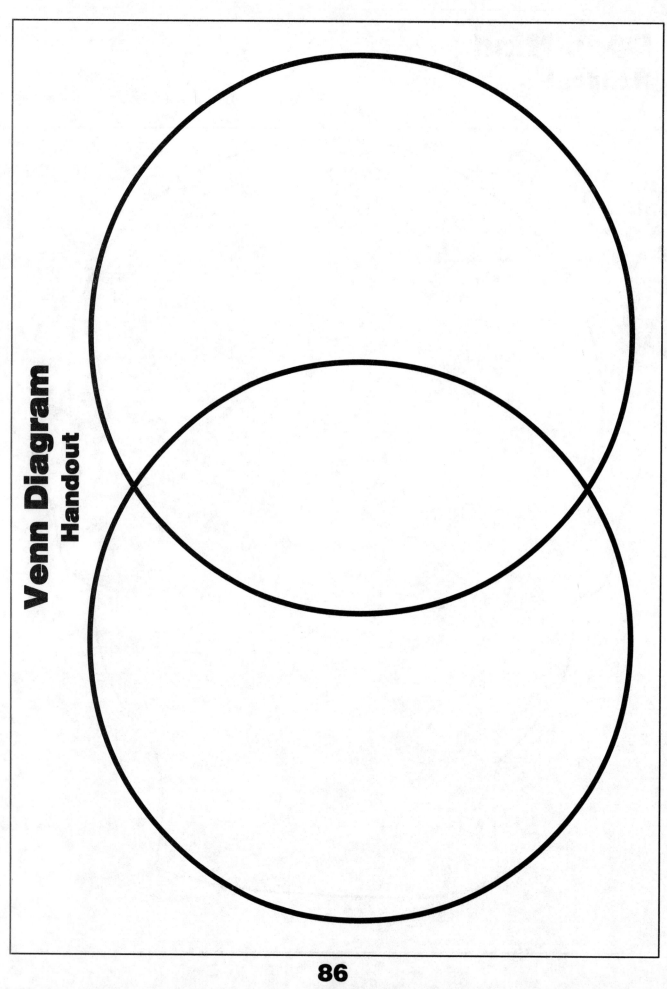

Venn Diagram
Handout

Double-Entry Journal
Handout

Qoutes	My Thoughts

Literary Report Card
Handout

For: _____
Name of Character

In: _____
Title of Book

Subject	Grade	Comments

Somebady Wanted But So
Handout

Somebody

Wanted

_____

_____

_____

_____

_____

_____

But

So

_____

_____

_____

_____

_____

_____

Somebady Wanted But So

Bibliography of Adult Books About Children's Anger

Aaron, Jane, *When I'm Angry (The Language of Parenting, 2)* (1998)

Akin, Terri, et al., *Helping Kids Manage Grief, Fear, and Anger* (2000)

Dentemaro, Christine and Kranz, Rachel, *Straight Talk About Anger* (1995)

Eastman, Meg, *Taming the Dragon in Your Child: Solutions for Breaking the Cycle of Family Anger* (1994)

Eggert, Leona L., *Anger Management in Youth: Stemming Aggression and Violence* (1994)

Goodenough, Florence Laura, *Anger in Young Children* (1931)

Frost, Helen, *Feeling Angry (Emotions)* (1998)

Huggins, Pat, and Huggins, Doug, *Helping Kids Handle Anger: A Validated Washington State Innovative Education Program* (1993)

Karres, Erica, V., et al., *Violence Proof Your Kids Now: How to Recognize the 8 Warning Signs and What to Do About Them* (2000)

Laforge, Ann E., *Tantrums: Secrets to Calming the Storm* (1996)

McCoy, Elin, *What to Do ... When Kids Are Mean To Your Child (What to Do Parenting Guides, Vol. 1)* (1997)

Myles, Brenda Smith, et al., *Asperger Syndrome and Difficult Moments: Practical Solutions for Tantrums, Rage and Meltdowns* (1999)

Porter, Daniel J., *Taming Monster Moments: Tips for Turning on Soul Light to Help Children Handle Fear and Anger (Creative Meditations for Children)* (1999)

Paul, Henry A., *When Kids Are Mad, Not Bad: A Guide to Recognizing and Handling Your Child's Anger* (1999)

Randolf, Gretchen, et al., *Danny and the Fiery Dragon* (1997)

Remboldt, Carole, *Helping Kids Resolve Conflicts Without Violence (Johnson Institute Resources for Parenting)* (1996)

Riley, Susan, *Angry (Thoughts and Feelings)*

Whitehouse, Elaine, and Pudney, Warwick, *A Volcano in My Tummy: Helping Children to Handle Anger* (2000)

Wilde, Jerry, *Hot Stuff to Help Kids Chill Out: The Anger Management Book* (1997)

Wilde, Jerry, *Anger Management in Schools* (1995)

Wood, Rose, *Dysinhibition Syndrome: How to Handle Anger and Rage in Your Child or Spouse* (1999)